Pre-school Learning in the Community

Strategies for change

G.A. Poulton and Terry James

Routledge
Taylor & Francis Group
ROUTLEDGE REVIVALS

First published in 1975
by Routledge & Kegan Paul Ltd

This edition first published in 2018 by Routledge
2 Park Square, Milton Park, Abingdon, Oxon OX14 4RN

and by Routledge
711 Third Avenue, New York, NY 10017

Routledge is an imprint of the Taylor & Francis Group, an informa business

Publisher's Note
The publisher has gone to great lengths to ensure the quality of this reprint but points out that some imperfections in the original copies may be apparent.

Disclaimer
The publisher has made every effort to trace copyright holders and welcomes correspondence from those they have been unable to contact.

A Library of Congress record exists under ISBN: 0710082452

ISBN: 978-1-138-48816-8 (hbk)
ISBN: 978-1-351-04162-1 (ebk)
ISBN: 978-1-138-48825-0 (pbk)

Routledge Revivals

Pre-school Learning in the Community

Much of current educational theory and research at the time was concerned with the effect that pre-school education should have in accelerating development throughout the years of compulsory schooling. This book, originally published in 1975, is an important contribution to the debate since it shows how the stages of pre-schooling affect the child, the family and the neighbourhood community.

The authors point out that pre-school stands at the intersection between the informal socialisation of the home and the more disciplined learning which takes place at school. Much research appears to show that poor progress in primary school results partly from adverse family circumstances; but it reveals just as plausibly that the formal measures of progress used by both the research and our schools are reflecting a limited view of progress and one which does least justice to the norms and values of families which do not share established academic goals. For this reason a cultural shock is experienced by many children on joining school. The authors argue that pre-school, as a transitional phase, could do much to reduce the shock, but that many of the efforts made for the under-fives simply expose them earlier to the contrast between home and school learning situations. They recognise that parents are educators and play a prominent part in the intellectual and social development of their children. They also stress that the effect of pre-school children on the social or psychological well-being of parents and children will be limited unless it takes account of and reaches out to the community to which they belong. The authors offer several alternative approaches to pre-school organisation and content of the time and examine some specific examples, such as the Pre-school Playgroup movement and the Leicester Home-Start scheme.

Pre-school learning in the community

Strategies for change

G. A. Poulton,
Extra-Mural Studies Department, Southampton University

and

Terry James,
Social Evaluation Unit, Oxford University

Routledge & Kegan Paul
London and Boston

First published in 1975
by Routledge & Kegan Paul Ltd
Broadway House, 68-74 Carter Lane,
London EC4V 5EL and
9 Park Street,
Boston, Mass. 02108, USA
Set in Journal by Autoset

ISBN 0 7100 8245 2 (c)
ISBN 0 7100 8246 0 (p)

Contents

Preface

The ideas and arguments contained in the following chapters arise from the authors' participation in several educational projects, including the Educational Priority Areas Project, which ran for three years during 1969-1971 and has been written up in *Educational Priority* edited by Dr A. H. Halsey, the director of the project.[1] Five action-research teams, working largely independently, applied and evaluated strategies which they found appropriate for educational priority areas (EPAs).

As members of the West Riding team, one of our major concerns was the operation of pre-school facilities set up by the project in the town on which it was based, in a South Yorkshire mining valley. The team had made the development of early education programmes a priority because it became apparent at a preliminary stage that to affect the educational experiences of pre-school aged children was a potential means of accelerating their development throughout the years of compulsory schooling. The power of pre-schooling to influence later development has been the subject of sceptical commentaries on the Head Start and similar programmes in the USA, from which the EPA project in Britain received a certain stimulus. The project's particular response to the American precedent and the degree of success with which the effects of its own programmes were maintained in the longer term, are shown in *Educational Priority*[2] and in further, unpublished, reports. Because the West Riding team had, with the generous assistance of the West Riding Education Authority, set up a social educational centre (Red House), the development of pre-school methodology was able to continue there beyond the end of the project. It is mainly from this later period that the authors' observations are drawn, since it was at this time that the Red House pre-school programme had reached its most articulated and stable form, accumulating the experience of the earlier pre-school programmes and adding to it the refinements which their continued development produced. It is also during this period, 1972–4, that preparations have been made by the government for the large-scale expansion of pre-school provision in England and Wales. Certain of the objectives for pre-schooling suggested by the Department of Education and Science[3] are shared by the programme at Red House. *A Framework for Expansion*[4] and Circular 2/73[5] refer to the need for educational content and parental collaboration in pre-school groups; there is an immediate antecedent to this suggestion in the structure of the Red House groups, which came to be known as hybrid pre-school groups because they combined the parents' participation generally found in privately and voluntarily organized playgroups with an educational component more commonly a feature of statutory nurseries.

The hybrid prototype, however, continues to develop; to these two main features must be added others which have emerged from a project in operation for five years to date, if the approaches which have been worked out and the warnings received in those groups are to be of service in the impending proliferation of pre-school provision.

The structures, practices and ideas which form the present examination of pre-schooling have been developed through contact with co-workers and critics too numerous to acknowledge individually, but we are grateful for the guidance of all those who visited or were in touch with Red House during its first four years, particularly the parents and children who supported the pre-school groups. We also gratefully acknowledge our colleagues who discussed and prepared the drafts and typescript. If any formula can summarize the observations made in the following pages it is this: pre-school strategies, while affecting the child and his family profoundly, are also parts of larger totalities and depend for their success on looking beyond the group to the social, political and education systems, both local and national, with which they interact. Pre-school education will have but limited effect on the social or psychological well-being of its customers—the parents and children—unless it takes account of and reaches out to the community to which they belong. It will have no power to provide the educational opportunities which can lead to increased life chances without a good deal of attention being given to the structure of those systems which regulate access to education and occupations.

The chapters which follow attempt to place pre-schooling in its theoretical and practical contexts. This is not undertaken in the spirit of an exhaustive review, however, which a number of other works, often cited in the text, achieve more fully. The present volume is, rather, an analysis, including a case study based on the authors' particular experiences, which emphasizes the socializing role of pre-school in the family and its neighbourhood.

In Chapter 1 some of the best, most reliable and relevant research evidence on the relationship between home background and educational attainment is examined. In Chapter 2 it is argued that that type of evidence, along with familiarity of certain programmes in the USA, has encouraged in Britain a compensatory approach to pre-school provision for underprivileged children which is not altogether appropriate. The difficulties in this approach and in alternative strategies are also discussed. Chapter 3 presents a graphic account of the day-to-day activities of the type of pre-school group which acts as a model for the suggestions being made about the possible role of a pre-school group within the community.

The content and structure implied by this type of provision are discussed in Chapters 4 and 5 which deal respectively with the impact it can have upon the child's learning processes and upon the social and educational environment in which he lives, that is, his family, his neighbourhood and the community services, including schools. Chapter 6 explores some early educational strategies other than pre-school groups which are making their own contributions to the fund of pre-school experience. In conclusion, the argument of the preceding chapters is reviewed and some of its implications for the immediate future of early education are drawn out.

Acknowledgments

Research and fieldwork in early education has accelerated and expanded rapidly in recent years. We acknowledge with gratitude the contributions of a number of authors and practitioners providing us with recent information and comment. In particular we are indebted to Margaret Harrison of Home Start, Leicester; Teresa Smith, Department of Social and Administrative Studies, Oxford University; Stella Lightman; Dr A. Lombard, Hebrew University of Jerusalem; and Dr Louise Sandler, Franklin Institute, Philadelphia. We are also grateful to Messrs Longmans Ltd; University of Chicago Press; Ontario Institute of Educational Studies, Toronto and Dr Marion Blank, for the use of copyright material.

Much of the case study contained in this volume centres around the work of many parents and children, together with Lin Poulton, Ann Seaton, Joan Davis, in the pre-school groups, while Gina Armstrong and Liz Worden pioneered educational home-visiting with a further group of parents.

Preparation of the typescript, always a difficult chore, was carried out with extreme efficiency and tolerance by Reba Lawless.

G.A.P.
T.E.J.

Southampton

Part 1

Research and development in early education

1

Criteria for success or failure

The impending expansion of pre-school facilities in this country partly reflects the importance which has come to be attached in recent years to two trends of thinking about children's development. One of these is the discovery, or rediscovery, of the fact that children can be exposed with benefit to instructional processes earlier than the school system operates. In the context of this book, this thinking requires little argumentation since it is self-evident that learning takes place from birth onwards; what is of more concern to us is the means by which the various learning processes to which the child is exposed are organized and are changing. This brings us to the second trend in thinking about children's development, which is the recognition of both family and school as socialization agencies of considerable significance in that development. Given that the home is an informal agency while schools are relatively formal, regularized institutions, then playgroups and nurseries naturally stand at a crucial and transitional stage in the continuous socialization process. This stage sharpens the more general relationship between home and school which has become the subject of a great deal of writing in the sociology of education, a discipline which has contributed the notion of cultural differences between homes and schools. The fact that there can exist differences between the prevailing educational climates presented to the child in the family on the one hand and the classroom on the other gives rise to potential conflicts and misunderstandings between teachers and parents which allow no straightforward resolution.

Belonging to a pre-school group, whether it is voluntarily organized or set up by the local authority, brings these possible disparities of approach into focus, but can also provide the opportunity for their successful combination in a process of teacher-parent collaboration. As with relations between the home and the primary school the informal and formal learning contexts may be in conflict with each other, or, given a combination of luck and circumstance, in harmony with each other. Luck is the opportunity that a parent has to find a local group, or school, which promises to develop, as well as act as custodian of, the child; or it is the teacher's chances of looking after children whose parents have some feeling about their children's development. Circumstance, as it is conducive to harmony between parent and teacher, is a matter of shared educational values; this can be a happy state unless the academic ambitions of the parent for the child are too demanding for his balanced development. Much of the literature of educational sociology is, however, devoted to studying the failure of the link between home and schools and has become particularly relevant to the provision of pre-school places, particularly places for the children of families who experience forms of disadvantage, especially the 'cultural disadvantage' which is taken to exist where the home's and the school's values are misaligned. Whatever the relevance of the concept of disadvantage in making educational provisions, a matter to be taken up shortly, it is at least true to say that not all families are equally well placed to prepare their children to take full advantage of the facilities offered by the formal education system.

The contribution of research

The influential cultural studies of education in Britain have tended to concentrate on social class differences in attainment or opportunity.[1] While these studies foreshadowed in several ways the current concern that education should take account of pupil's background and circumstances, their emphasis was differently placed. The general effect of these British studies in educational sociology was to draw attention to inequalities of educational opportunity between social strata: children of middle-class parents were found to have greater than average chances of obtaining grammar-school places, of performing well in examinations, of using linguistic codes which assisted their progress through academic and professional life, and so on. Valuable as such findings are especially for highlighting the effects on selection procedures for secondary and higher education, they offer little help to the professional educator since they offer few clues to what it is about working-class membership or cultures that has this apparently inhibiting and cumulative effect. Rather more sophisticated sociological analyses would be required to investigate those effects. Concentrating on problems of the outcomes of education, rather than access to it, other more recent studies have attempted to locate specific causes of underachievement by relating large numbers of background and circumstantial variables to performance on psychological or attainment tests. The rationale of these surveys has been to explain levels and variation in test scores in terms of a number of presumed influences from the child's domestic, personal and school situations. The difficulties about using such results for reform are fairly evident, and the studies can only approximately be described as a form of sociological analysis; yet this type of research seems to have had a remarkable effect upon the course of home/school strategies and upon thinking about the sources of failure at school. It seems to us that as well as overestimating the home's contribution to achievement in school, surveys have often given rise to optimistic expectations about the applicability of their findings. If it were discovered, for instance, from a survey of home circumstances and reading ability that the type of education received by the parents, the number of books they kept at home and how much television the family watched each day had, on aggregate, an influence on reading achievement or progress in school, then in all probability an actual relationship between these variables exists. Empirical findings such as these can make valuable contributions to theory and are viable in policy discussions; however, their value in designing strategies or arguing for deliberate reforms is limited by certain methodological difficulties, the chief of which are as follows.

Findings such as those being discussed relate to a historical context from which it is invalid to predict that they will apply in a new context; it may be, for instance, that an association is discovered between low average achievement and large school classes, or large schools, or large head teachers, for that matter. It does not follow that a deliberate change of size will result in higher average achievements for the pupils, because the relationship between size and achievement is unlikely to be directly causal, or so simple that variation in the one completely explains variation in the other.

As well as the fact of causality, the direction of causation is difficult to establish. For instance, if families' educational aspirations for their children were found to be associated with the children's performance, it is not clear whether performance affects aspirations or vice versa, or whether all levels of performance, high and low, are involved in the relationship, or indeed whether there is a mutual feedback process operating between aspirations and performance. Any attempt to improve children's performance by affecting their families' aspirations could, on the strength of this evidence alone, turn out to be not the most efficient approach, and (since the evidence takes account neither of the direction of causation nor of different levels of aspiration and performance) possibly counter-productive in some cases.

To attain reasonable reliability, survey findings need to be generalized over large portions of the sample, which therefore needs to be large itself; there will tend to be many individual cases in which the discovered relationship does not hold. Unfortunately, the probability that a majority will benefit is not always a good recommendation for reform (as for instance, when an otherwise effective vaccine produces a fatal reaction in 1 per cent of the population). An example from the educational field would be the (fictitious) finding that most children achieve greater social adjustment in nursery classes if the room is noisy and active rather than in quiet rows of desks. If applied indiscriminately, a policy of noise and activity might have a quite unexpected result for children with agoraphobic tendencies, unexpected, that is, if one truly believed that the same conditions could be ideal for every child.

Sometimes factors may be identified which have a strong association with each other but either the relationship or the factors themselves are not readily amenable to change. Children's performance and father's socio-economic status are often said to stand in such a relationship. Here the relationship is presumably not very direct but operates through the mediating effect of attitudes and predispositions that are themselves often associated with socio-economic status; perhaps the kind of indirect relationship indicates a further type of fallacy which is possible in interpreting research findings, that of ignoring 'intervening variables'. The main point of this example, however, is to show how a quite powerful determinant is out of reach for reform purposes. In other words, changing jobs will not, of itself, ensure an increase in one's children's academic performance, although it may indirectly achieve that result in some cases by affecting the intervening variables too. It is no good to overeat if you want to gain height, even though there is in the population as a whole a strong tendency for the tallest to be the heaviest. If households with no inside toilets or hot running water tend to produce underachieving children then converting corridors into bathrooms will not boost achievement, although it may be a possible beginning in ameliorating depressive living conditions.

Possibly the first directly influential survey report in the field in question was the national survey conducted for the Plowden committee and published in volume 2 of *Children and their Primary Schools.*[2] This report is significant also in this discussion for its almost direct impact on the subsequent development of compensatory strategies in primary education (the educational priority areas) and in the encouragement of parents' involvement in earlier education. Probably all of the difficulties listed above apply to using that study as a guide to action; there have, in addition, been several published criticisms of the Plowden committee's findings[3] and its surveys.[4] It is difficult to endorse all these criticisms but attention should be drawn to the method of statistical analyses used in the survey (stepwise multiple regression), which has a particular effect on the results connected with parental influence.

The list of 'explanatory' variables, which were expected to account for a large proportion of the variation in the test scores of primary school children, were grouped empirically into school factors, teachers' characteristics, home circumstances and parents' aspirations and encouragement. By establishing the contribution of parental factors first, then determining the proportion of the remaining variation in test score which was attributable to the other groups of variables taken in order, it follows that maximum estimates of parental contributions were obtained. The groups of variables were taken in chronological order of presumed influence on attainment, parents' and home factors having prior claim. If the contributions of all factors were taken at once, quite probably some parental and home circumstances would still account statistically for a fair proportion of the variation, but the teachers' and schools' shares would increase. There seems little justification for allowing parental and home factors to absorb variation first, leaving less for other types of influence. Even that which is due to domestic factors will almost certainly operate partly through teachers, who perceive and react to children's home backgrounds: several studies (see especially Pidgeon[5] who reviews many of them) have demonstrated the quite strong effects of teachers' perceptions of background characteristics upon pupils' progress or performance.

It would be churlish to deny that important relationships between parents' aspirations, home circumstances and the children's school attainments exist; but it is possible that evidence has been presented by the Plowden study, and others which support it, which exaggerates parental influence at the expense of other factors. Some of these other factors have been taken into account, such as teachers' and schools' characteristics, and some, like the values of the local education system or the resources available relatively to the rest of the country, have not generally been considered. More importantly, underlying the home's and parents' power over children's development, there may often be a range of cultural factors which either restrict or maximize the potential educational development of children; or rather they appear to affect development, for the causal chain between cultural background and educational attainment cannot, in the nature of the phenomena, be direct, and will consist of many intermediate links. Many of the cultural factors are well recognized because of the publicity attracted by studies of attainment and family background, especially those factors which are claimed to restrict the relative progress of children from poor or uneducated homes by depressing standards of living, and by curbing aspirations and motivations, on the part of parents, children, and of teachers, too.

The limitations of survey evidence which were noted above will restrict the value of studies which relate children's backgrounds to their development in the process of policy formulation, and undoubtedly popular misconceptions have arisen which continue to affect thinking on the cultural aspects of psychological and physical growth. With careful interpretation, nevertheless, the research can offer useful insights. Rather than reject altogether the contribution of research to understanding in this field, it would be wise to examine the most detailed and careful research available, to see what it has to say on the subject of home influences, and to consider if there are any indications for fruitful action. The most comprehensive study in recent years of development and its concomitant variables has been the National Child Development Study carried out by the National Children's Bureau.

The National Child Development Study

The development and background of the 17,418 children who were born in England, Wales and Scotland between 3 and 9 March 1958, or rather as many of them who could be traced and had survived to the age of seven, were the chief objects of investigation in this study.[6] Surveys at two points in time (at birth and at 7 ye rs) had been conducted, and further follow-up surveys were planned at 11 and 15 years, so that the study has a valuable longitudinal feature. The study is one of impressive administrative efficiency which achieved an amazingly high response rate from the children, their parents and their teachers seven years after the sample was originally drawn: just under 16,000 provided information at seven years old and over 14,000 at both birth and the age of seven. The study considers both physical and psychological characteristics at the age of seven and constructs predictive models which are intended to link these with antecedent circumstances at birth or with the conditions in existence at seven in the family or at school.

While the prediction of physical development by factors surrounding birth is generally on safe ground because of the longitudinal character of the study, the arguments for relating family circumstances to psychological development rely on evidence gathered at one point in time; further follow-up surveys will overcome this difficulty to a large extent.

The social background factors whose relationship with development are investigated include: family size, parents' education and social origins, parental interest in their children's education, the parental situation, whether the mother works, family moves, household amenities and overcrowding. National, regional, social class and sex differences are also investigated, and so too are behaviour at home and school. It is more or less true to say that each of these variables is found to have some kind of bearing, not always very direct, upon achievement and adjustment at seven years old.

The formal measures used to assess achievement and adjustment and to relate them to circumstances were the Southgate reading test, a problem arithmetic test and the Bristol Social Adjustment Guide. The Goodenough 'draw-a-man' test was used but not reported in that volume. The choice of measures is a point of critical importance in our argument since it has had profound implications for the way in which the study's findings have been used in subsequent policy discussions and reviews; for the two achievement tests are, perhaps inevitably, very strongly related to major primary school objectives, and furthermore, they embody middle-class values as the report makes clear:

> Attainment tests at best measure reliably what the author of the test and its users judge to be desirable. Most tests of intelligence are designed essentially to predict future performance in school work . . . . Teachers, research workers and others must use some framework as a basis for evaluation. That the framework embodies ideas, attitudes and expectations which are more commonly met in middle-class homes and therefore amongst middle-class children, is perhaps inevitable in our society (p.29).

The Bristol Social Adjustment Guide is even more evidently biased towards the teacher's point of view since it consists entirely of teachers' ratings of a child's social behaviour in school; what the teacher perceives as appropriate social adjustment may very easily consist in behaviour which is more convenient when handling a (possibly overcrowded) classroom.

The researchers' approach to the problem of a cultural bias in the measures is to suggest that since none can be 'culture-free' it does no good to throw them away and that they should be used with reservations. Unfortunately reservations have a habit of being overlooked in commentaries on research studies, and something of the sort has happened, but more of this later.

There are some further aspects of the study which limit the possible interpretations put on the data in a way which has been largely ignored, even though the limitations were in most cases pointed out by the authors, and some of them are very similar to those general limitations of survey data noted earlier.

1 The choice of variables on which to collect information naturally imposes restrictions on possible findings. Apart from the tests and assessments of children, the information fell mainly into the categories of family circumstances and practices, physiological conditions, and school organization. An area not within the study's scope was the neighbourhood and community environment in which the child lived, although the authors frequently achnowledge the significance of such factors. Apart from these large portions of (necessarily) unaccounted-for influences on achievement, there is the possibility that the variables which are included are 'standing in' for other, possibly more direct, influences on the person-to-person (e.g. mother-to-child) level with which they are statistically related in the sample. These two possibilities imply that there may be powerful determinants of achievement not accounted for by the study.

2 The type of analysis which is applied to the data also affects the findings. Some acknowledgment is given in the report that there may be influential groups of factors related to, but not completely identified with, home circumstances, by including father's occupation as an explanatory variable in the analyses. This variable, renamed 'social class' in the report, is claimed to represent a set of influences whose composition is largely unknown but which together possess great power in explaining differential achievement. In many of the analyses presented, the presumed effects of single variables upon achievement or adjustment are estimated after other variables in that set have been taken into account. Sets of variables which empirically hang together are taken and 'social class' is included in many of those sets so that the separate influence of father's occupation can be omitted from the remaining influences; frequently, father's occupation absorbs more variation than other variables in the set, showing that it represents an important correlate of the various tests and assessments. Plainly the work a father does (or rather the way in which it is classified by the Registrar General) cannot normally affect his son's or daughter's school career other than indirectly, through, for instance, the father's

educational attitudes and through the reactions which others, such as the child and his or her friends, and teachers, have toward the father's attitudes and occupational status. Many more links between job and children's progress could no doubt be found by appropriate methods of enquiry, and, if they could be adequately quantified, would presumably exert a similar influence to 'social class' in the National Child Development Study; the point being made (because it is easily forgotten) is that the factor which appears to explain so much does so only obscurely. As the report says on page 27: 'Family and home influences operate in complex and subtle ways. The analysis of the material can take some account of these complexities but a large-scale study is not well equipped to search out subtleties.'

3 Even more tractable variables suffer the same kind of difficulty as the surrogate 'social class': the instance of household amenities is mentioned below. The only variables which are relatively free of interpretative difficulties are the birth and health items, which are nevertheless treated to essentially the same forms of analysis and reporting. In two very similar analyses, for instance, variables such as age of mother at child's birth, increase in birth-weight, smoking during pregnancy and 'social class' are mixed in the same regression analysis, first to predict child's height (p. 82), and later (p. 176) to predict increase in reading age. Although similar and important statistical relationships may be found in the two analyses, the medical finding requires a different kind of interpretation to the educational one, where the chains of causality, if any, are likely to possess different kinds of, possibly more, links, each giving pause for speculation. It is easier to imagine a direct causal link between birth order and height than between lack of hot running water in the household and a child's reading attainment. The investigations required to demonstrate these relationships may be equally difficult to arrange, but the physiological example accords more closely with both common sense and theoretical models of how causation is defined. On p. 57 the report comments:

> It would, of course, be naive to assume a direct causal relationship between, say, lack of hot water in the household and children's reading attainment. But poor housing conditions may well lead to a low standard of physical health; depression and irritability in parents; and may produce a feeling of distance from the more privileged sections of society (with which the school may be identified). Thus, a combination of adverse environmental circumstances may well have a deleterious effect on children's development.

This passage demonstrates well the tortuous accounts which can be involved in explaining social science findings; in particular, it shows how factors extraneous to the study are drawn in and how questions arise about which factors influence which others. The possibility that the circumstances termed 'adverse' may affect the perceptions and treatment to which a child is subject at school, a possibility which would complicate the explanation considerably, is not even introduced.

4 Inevitably, in discussing the interaction between school achievements and family background, considerable attention becomes directed toward the problems of underachievement and adverse background factors. In spite of the fact that the underachievement occurs on tests and assessments which reflect the school's rather than the family's or child's requirements, and in spite of the fact that the causal links between background conditions and achievement cannot be satisfactorily explained, nevertheless the underachieving children are termed 'disadvantaged' and the phenomenon is attributed to the conditions rather than to the children or to the education system which prescribes the forms and levels of achievement to be striven for, or to the interaction of all these (as well, doubtless, as many more) components.

Again it is easier to comprehend how physical handicap or birth factors can influence physical, or even psychological development, than how family environment can influence attainments. In fact the report makes a fairly clear distinction between (physical or mental) handicap and (educational or social) disadvantage; it attempts a serious predictive exercise of selectively screening for children at risk only in the medical sphere. When considering the influence of conditions of a more domestic nature, the authors suggest sociological explanations of achievement, but it is left to later commentaries to elevate these explanations to the less speculative realm of remedial prescriptions. The following quotations from *From Birth to Seven* illustrate the relative emphases placed by its authors upon the sociological and the medical predictive models:

> The identification in the survey and elsewhere of these and other high risk groups[7] has made possible more concentration of medical resources upon mothers in most need . . . (p. 10).

> No method of prediction can act as a substitute for actual examination of children but it can at least show the areas where maximum benefit, in terms of the detection of handicap, will result when preferential allocation of resources is made (p. 187).

> The results have demonstrated clearly the relationships between poor housing amenities and overcrowding on the one hand and on the other hand educational performance and social adjustment in school at the age of seven . . . . However, an improvement in housing conditions and other environmental circumstances cannot be achieved overnight, and so attention needs to be given to ways of ameliorating their effects. The Plowden Committee suggested a programme of compensation through 'educational priority areas'. Such schemes are unlikely to be fully effective until the ways in which children are influenced by adverse environmental circumstances are better understood. Further research in this area, therefore, is urgently needed (p. 57).

The first quotation is in fact a description of the system of 'selective screening' referred to earlier, which allows scarce resources for medical examination to be placed optimally to pick up children who run a risk of later handicap—a risk which is demonstrated statistically and presumed to be predictable. In the second quotation the notion of 'positive discrimination' is presented; it is strikingly analogous to selective screening, but because of the vagueness of the predictive relationships involved, the authors are judiciously sceptical about its immediate application. They can hardly be accused of ignoring the limitations of their findings in this respect.

5 Perhaps inevitably, opinions about desirable changes in policy and approach do overlay the technical reporting of the study. On the low take-up of welfare services of various kinds on the part of those presumed to be most in need, the report says: 'Whatever the reasons it is important that these should be uncovered and understood and that services should seek, wherever necessary, to adapt in order to meet the needs of all their "clients" ' (p.192). The finger is also pointed at parents: 'To the extent that [regional] differences [in educational attainment] are a function of community or parental attitudes it is important to isolate and study these attitudes so that parents can be made aware of their relevance to children's attainments' (p. 111). And again, when underachievers in large families are being discussed:

> Amongst larger families which are not planned in size, apart from those where religious considerations predominate, there is likely to be a higher proportion of parents whose attitude is rather feckless and irresponsible, those who in general do not manage their affairs very successfully and those who tend to live for the present (p. 34).

It is made clear, however, that these parents and children will tend to have a scale of values which contrasts quite sharply with what has been described as 'the middle-class ethic of postponed gratification' (p. 34), and that 'children from large families are at a considerable disadvantage in school' (p. 35). Schools, too, are given a cross to bear: '. . . schools can perhaps help by compensating for any retardation of verbal skills and concepts in the classroom programme' (p. 35).

Leaving aside the problem that this latter comment is based on reading, not verbal, attainment, there is some recognition, then, that part of the problem of underachievement is properly the schools'. The suggestion is that the verbal (or reading) skills of disadvantaged children are not only different but also retarded, and so they are, but in terms of the formal standards used both in the tests and generally in schools. The study recognizes the possibilities of cultural conflict between school staff who are middle-class by definition (p. 137) and the parents of disadvantaged children. This recognition is quite rightly limited to the findings, which deal with visits to the school by parents and with parent-teacher associations. There is not, nor can be, perhaps, any scope within the framework of the study for investigating the infant school's ability to accommodate the variety of its intake; it is rather the variation of that intake which is studied. This format naturally limits the recommendations which can be made for schools. Perhaps the only concrete policy recommendation which impinges directly on the teacher is that pupils with spectacles should sit near the front of a classroom. It is to be hoped that teachers will not be too eager to follow slavishly such advice if they happen to arrange their children's workspace without a 'front', and without directing them to assigned places.

The example of the National Child Development Study has been dwelt on at some length in order to make clear the nature of the evidence on which many recent recommendations and actions in the field of domestic influences on learning in young children have been based. It is, of course, not the only relevant study in the field, but none is as recent,[8] or based on a large, almost complete national sample of children in the early stages of compulsory education. These conditions enable us to feel fairly certain of the relative contributions of the factors included in the study to the educational criteria which it employed; the fact that the contributions of more wide-ranging factors within the educational, social and economic systems have not been estimated are not the fault of the study; they remain in a realm of speculation and argument to which other studies and writings can lend partial but necessarily inconclusive support. A final quotation from the Foreword of *From Birth to Seven* makes just this point: 'The patterns glimpsed in the National Child Development Study are so deeply embedded in this country's economic and social structure that they cannot be greatly changed by anything short of equally far-reaching changes in that structure.'

A pattern of disadvantage

In the light of studies such as the National Child Development Study, which have investigated the relationship between home and education, particular attention has been drawn to the problems of disadvantaged sectors of the population and the tendency for the children to fall behind in achievement and adjustment, in their educational or occupational careers. Accompanying this development have been attempts to find strategies for intervening in the connection between disadvantaged circumstances and lack of success in school and afterwards.[9] Very often, and for reasons explored later, those strategies have concentrated on parents and children at a time before compulsory formal education begins, but sometimes on schools as well. Few strategies affect the link between family and school, and indeed this would appear a difficult result to achieve.

In discussing the National Child Development Study it became evident that the connection between disadvantage and underachievement had a lot to do with the ways in which the two concepts are defined. Achievement, and to an even greater extent adjustment, were assessed according to strongly school-related criteria, and disadvantage was conceived in terms of the difficulties which the child faced in attending school and conforming to its norms. A child may be disadvantaged at school by his background; it would be inaccurate in the light of the available evidence to say that the child for that reason came from a disadvantaged background. The point of this apparent quibble is to show how emphasis can come to be placed upon the background as an object for remediation rather than upon the schools and the socializing system they embody, or upon the interaction between schools and the cultural background of the children in their care.

Emphasis upon the home rather than the education system or the reaction of each to the other as the prime source of cultural conflict has, it seems, frequently been taken for granted as being the appropriate point of attack when recommending policies and programmes for remedying the situation. Two particular developments in the debate have contributed to the home being singled out as the appropriate object of attention in many intervention projects and policies. On the one hand the sources of disadvantage which are located in the family have been built into a concept of 'deprivation' which is itself reckoned to impede a child's career. On the other hand the potential which schools possess for redressing the balance of the differential achievement of children from various backgrounds has been valued very lowly. The idea that schools produce little of the variation in their pupils' performance appears to be supported by the analyses of the Plowden survey data in which the school factors contribute far less to performance than parental attitudes and home circumstances. The decision, referred to earlier, to enter the parental and home factors first into the analyses would exaggerate their influence. Furthermore, the representation of reading test score by a school average for the children sampled, in an analysis which estimates the influence of school factors on score, may underestimate the variability in individual scores which is due to schools. It seems likely, too, that the actual range of variation in the school factors will be restricted compared with differences between parents or homes, so that there is greater scope for family influences than for school factors to be associated with children's achievements. As the interpretative comments of the Plowden survey noted, school factors comprise teachers' characteristics and school methods and organization, all of which conform to a certain minimum standard, whereas parents' circumstances and attitudes represent the complete available spectrum. The Coleman report from the USA[10] also found schools to be a relatively small source of variation in performance. There is no need to conclude, however, as many commentators have been led to believe, that schools make no difference: without formal educational arrangements average attainments on (especially school-based) criteria would almost certainly be much lower, while the variability due to variations in home background would remain high, probably even higher. Conversely, improvements in the school system may be capable of increasing average performance and reducing variability (or increasing the equality of educational output) although drafting such improvements and putting them into practice is another problem.

There is a second, more serious, contribution to the theory that the attack on inequality of educational opportunity should be centred on deprivation in the child's background rather than on reducing the cultural gap between schools and homes by influencing teachers. This is the belief that improving the background will affect educational achievement, which is implicit in many proposals for reform, and explicit in some, but would seem to stand very little chance of success, however good a thing it may be in itself, and however valid one's belief in a 'cycle of deprivation'. It has been commented earlier that changing the factors associated with underachievement cannot directly, of itself, affect achievement. It is possible that some effect may be felt indirectly, operating via changes in teachers' and parents' morale and perceptions of children's abilities. The relationship between home background and children's achievements is not sufficiently simple to be amenable to change of this kind, because it cannot be demonstrated in the first place that the discovered associations are of the cause-and-effect type and in the second place that a deliberate or encouraged change in the former would bring about the expected change in the latter. Too many assumptions have to be made about intervening and extraneous variables being negligible, and about the new, influenced situation being similar in its operational features to the one studied.

Despite these assumptions, which we have been at pains to point out are very probably unrealistic, they have constantly been risked in policy statements. Contemporaneously with the publication of *From Birth to Seven* the manuscript was given over to 'experienced and distinguished groups of practitioners, administrators and academics' to draw out its policy and practical implications. The dissemination of research findings to those on whom they impinge is often a difficult and inefficient process in the field of the social sciences, so that the desire to produce a short account which spelled out the implications was to be welcomed. Unfortunately, certain of the important provisos of the original study were omitted or ignored in the eventual publication of this account.[11] The most significant of these is the use of the term 'effect' to describe the relationship between circumstances and achievement without qualification, whereas the full report strenuously precludes interpretations involving causation. On p. 11, for instance, the booklet says:

> If the report is right in saying that parents' education can have important effects on children's development, the policy conclusion must be that parental education (in the fullest sense) to improve attitudes towards their children's education is of high importance.

In the light of our previous discussion it is apparent that the above statement combines two fallacies with a speculative leap; there is also an error in reporting the study's findings. One fallacy is the presumption that parents' education can affect children's development; the other is that altering the antecedent will affect the consequence in the intended way. The leap involved is to maintain that attitude modification will be possible in a way which will affect children's development. The error is contained in the identification of the study's 'parental education' factor, which was, in fact, school-leaving age, with the factor of parental education being recommended as a policy in this passage, which turns out to be an attempt to improve parents' attitudes. It is not that 'parental education (in the fullest sense)' is to be decried out of hand, but rather that no research evidence was available on which validly to base such a conclusion, so that the idea stands or falls on its own merits and appeal, rather than on the research findings which are claimed to support it. Other interesting policy recommendations, having varying degrees of basis in the study's findings, could be cited. One passage (p.10) makes the value-orientations of the educational recommendations fairly clear:

> The built-in bias in favour of middle-class children and the knowledge that 'there is no such thing as a culture-free test' reinforce the need for educational policies that will in particular compensate children from unskilled working-class homes but also, of course, children anywhere whose home conditions make successful educational progress difficult. We need more playgroups, nursery classes and educational discrimination in favour of children whose families cannot give them the orientation and the know-how in manipulating concepts that many middle-class families can provide. Secondly, teachers need to be more sensitive about the disadvantages of some children and the wariness with which 'objective' tests should be approached. Thirdly, parental education to close the gap between home and school needs to be more positively pursued.

The booklet goes on to mention that 'all these policies were called for by the Plowden Report'. In this passage we have some recognition of the roles both school and home play in producing unmatched expectations. Teachers are warned that tests may discriminate against the disadvantaged; it is not clear however, whether it is being acknowledged that the culture-loaded aspect of the tests has itself moulded the report's findings, and that moreover the term 'educational disadvantage' arises from the very fact that certain children (often from backgrounds which might be labelled 'deprived') do badly on such tests. The use of the word 'compensate' makes it clear where resources are being directed: the intention is that they should be invested in making children, parents and home backgrounds conform more closely to the requirements of the educational system rather than vice versa.

By the time the initial results were published from the second follow-up of the National Child Development Study,[12] the concept of social disadvantage had entered the orthodoxy of public debate on educational and social policy. Factors in children's home backgrounds which first came into prominence on the strength of their proven association with low achievement and difficult adjustment in schools, were in this report, and in much of the comment and official policy formation which followed it, given the role of social ills which deserved attention and amelioration on educational grounds.

Born to Fail? appears as a hard-hitting, deliberate popularization of the issues involved in the preliminary findings of the follow-up study of the sample children in 1969 when they were eleven years old; the booklet was thin, George Clarke's thirty photographs having an impact probably equal to the short text in the minds of many readers. The message contained in the text is that more eleven-year-olds than we are accustomed to think live in certain underprivileged conditions, and that membership of such a group is associated with many further unfortunate circumstances, including domestic factors, health, social background and behaviour and educational attainment. The argument is built up as follows. First three sets of family circumstances were impressionistically selected: family composition (i.e. a large number of children or only one parent figure), low income (i.e. child receiving free school meals or family in receipt of supplementary benefit during the previous year), and poor housing (i.e. a density of more than 1½ persons per room, or no sole use of hot water supply). Second, the authors calculated the proportion of the sample of children who came from families belonging to all three of the groups defined as above; the estimate obtained was 6 per cent, or one in sixteen, and this sector was termed 'socially disadvantaged'. The main body of the report is given over to explaining what proportion of the socially disadvantaged group are subject to certain other adverse conditions. These associated conditions, summarized broadly, include adverse birth factors, ill health and poor physical development, household amenities and accommodation, family's social background and education, and its use of the personal social services, parents' educational background, interest and aspirations, child's behaviour and attainment in school, conditions in the school, and child's history of pre-school attendance.

In each case, not unexpectedly, more socially disadvantaged children than 'advantaged' are found to be located in the poorly situated families. In some cases (for instance, physical development), what decides the 'poorly situated' category is fairly self-evident, while in others (household amenities and parents' education, for instance), a certain amount of subjectivity intrudes. In still further cases, such as behaviour and attainment in school, attendance at pre-school, and use of the social services, the decision is almost entirely judgmental as to what is a deficit or disadvantage and what is not. Whatever the case the upshot of this analysis is to describe a set of statistically and perhaps empirically linked circumstances, attainment being one of them, which powerfully suggest a pattern of disadvantage.[13] Remembering from the earlier evidence of *From Birth to Seven* that such circumstances were necessarily a disadvantage only in terms of school-based criteria, we should qualify the phrase as 'a pattern of educational disadvantage'; the fact that the circumstances themselves can be summed up as social ones merely describes them and does not prescribe the unique origin of the problem of disadvantage. The circumstances, once certain judgments have been made about them, may be considered 'deprived' and worthy in their own right of the attention of reformists. However well the set of deprived circumstances can be shown to hang together empirically both among themselves and with socio-economic status, attention to them will not necessarily affect the problem of underachievement and maladjustment in school as intended, nor lead to effective strategies for handling relations between families and the educational provisions which they use.

2

Intervention and innovation

Learning efficiency, or learning problems, among pre-schoolers and infants probably has very little directly to do with material or social deprivation. In Chapter 1 it was argued, from the evidence of a major British survey of background and achievement, that school performance at seven years of age cannot be explained in a way which is conducive to understanding and to policy, by reference to a child's family circumstances: for one thing those aggregated research findings are little help to teachers in solving individual children's learning problems, and for another they offer no causal explanations of success or failure at infant school which might be applicable in designing strategies and formulating policy.

There are some indications, even in the sources cited in Chapter 1, that school achievement and adjustment, in so far as they are related to pupils' backgrounds, are a function not only of those backgrounds, but also of the criteria used to measure success or failure. The measures used, even if they are technically well constructed tests or scales, do not take account of differences in pupils' cultural backgrounds to any great extent: this is almost bound to be true of any school-oriented tests or assessments. The idea that poor achievement or adjustment is often a joint function of school and home (in so far as it is a social phenomenon at all, and leaving the child's independent characteristics out of consideration for the moment) is further evidence of the existence of a 'cultural gap' between schools' objectives and the values of families and communities of those children who do not perform well according to the schools' objectives. As *Born to Fail?*[1] points out, in discussing the National Child Development Study's sample:

> Only one in 25 of the disadvantaged was middle class; the overwhelming majority was working class. Hence part of their failure to 'succeed' arises from the differences between their own language, values and experience of life and those implicitly or explicitly put forward by the school.

Currently, the existence of such a cultural gap is scarcely ever denied, but how it is perceived has large repercussions on the strategies and policies put forward for reducing its effects. Most frequently, teachers and administrators see the cultural backgrounds of poor achievers as falling short of the motivational and intellectual requirements of the academic curriculum. The above passage continues, however, quoting the Halsey report,[2] by pointing out that the expectations of schools are not necessarily appropriate goals for all children.

> 'not only must parents understand schools, schools must also understand the families and environments in which the children live . . . . Teachers need to be sensitive to the social and moral climate in which their children are growing up.' The [Halsey] report argues for the application of teaching to 'a compassionate, tolerant and critical examination of all social, political and moral issues' but regards this as 'the highest hurdle along the road to a community-oriented curriculum. It could take years and it will require a sympathetic and generous change of heart, not only among education authorities but in society at large.'

There are, it seems clear, great potential advantages to young children's learning and development, in effecting some kind of adjustment between the often conflicting expectations of teachers and parents. But what strategies are appropriate to the requirements of children? There is little point in labelling either the school or the home environment impoverished when it leads to an attack on one set of values or the other. When the home is seen as something to be compensated for, the risk is that the child's specific cultural bases of experience and learning will be ignored. On the other hand, when the formal educational system is seen as being irrevocably dissociated from the child's natural habitat a breaking down of the school's values is sometimes advocated, so that only 'culturally relevant' elements will be permitted in the curriculum, or, at the extreme, the abolition of schools as institutions will be proposed. Thus, by de-schooling, or by denying the professional teacher any power in managing schools, one forgoes many of the consequences of a formalized system, such as the idea of training for required standards for entrance to certain occupations and training, or the notion of a basic minimum of skills and abilities for general use in social and occupational life. While not decrying, or even rejecting, the destruction of educational systems as a solution—after all the balance of power lies greatly in the schools' favour at the present—it is beyond the scope and beside the point of our present discussion. In this volume the suggestion is being made, with such evidence and arguments as we can muster, that unilateral attacks on either schools' or families' values may be misplaced or inefficient. Proposals which require an attitude change on the part of either or both institutions are more promising but a little utopian. More realistic would be an effort to lead teachers and the families they serve into a greater physical and social proximity, facilitating interaction on the levels of cultural and educational values.

More than any other finding the significant but mistermed 'social class effect' on attainment indicates the cultural roots of ability to learn. It also prompts further enquiry into the precise mechanisms which lie behind the family's power to determine part of its children's learning ability. As always, further research is needed to clarify the interaction of family and learning, and indeed there are more intensive relevant and necessarily smaller-scale studies than the surveys quoted in the previous chapter which attack the problem.[3] Such small-scale research is essentially piecemeal and its justification is that it contributes to general theory; it can get closer to the operational aspects of family life which influence children's learning and can in part avoid the limitations of using simple objective tests by applying a battery of measures which includes in-depth attitude and personality material. Unfortunately, small-scale projects can rarely be comprehensive enough to locate sets of circumstances which are important to development and socialization; it remains a matter of interpreting evidence available from many sources, and this will inevitably include an element of speculation.

An alternative to compensation

The fact that many of the aims of compensatory education may be based on incomplete evidence does not in itself mean that they are ill-conceived, particularly given the unlikelihood of better evidence coming to hand. It is on ideological as well as pedagogic grounds that educational objectives are set up and maintained. Choices of curriculum and content, of structure and syllabus and whether these shall be fixed according to the needs of an educational élite or those of the catchment area, are explicable from the results of social analysis at least as much as from those of educational research. Where it is a question of early socialization, anthropological concepts figure also. Educational disadvantage itself is rooted in social stratification. The goals of formal socialization are the products of value systems which have evolved out of the more general social and economic structures, and thus tend to be associated with the socially and economically dominant cultures; the aims of education, in other words, derive from those of a social élite. The less formal socialization processes, those which operate in family and neighbourhood, will tend to be seen by the dominant professional groups as alternative, sometimes deviant, cultures, which are therefore under-represented in the formal education system.

The frequent failure of formal education systems to accommodate cultures which have different emphases from their own, manifests itself partly in the educational outcomes for pupils and schools. Outcomes in terms of pupil ability hit their lowest averages in schools where the generalized academic culture is at odds with that of the catchment area. There may, of course, be good reasons for insisting on the maintenance of standards in the academic syllabus in areas where national norms are difficult to achieve; after all, children who are likely to leave school with no useful qualifications, it could be argued, are in especial need of basic literacy and numeracy. It is also a point worth making, even though it cannot help the unqualified early drop-out from the educational system, that the contents of the higher reaches of specialized training are culturally determined to only a minimal extent, and from these upper reaches most formal educational objectives flow. Whatever the justice of that point of view, at least it must be admitted by advocates of community education, that the 'culturally-relevant curriculum' recedes in importance among specialist disciplines; socially relevant applications, naturally, remain important. The point at issue is that for the under-fives in educational institutions the pressure of academic criteria of progress is at a minimum. Unless pre-school groups become nothing more than a downward extension of school, the limits on children's expressive and instructive activity can be virtually ignored: parents and teachers can together help children to find their own rates and routes of exploration; a programme of activities can be undertaken which bases development and cognition upon the child's primary experiences of the immediate neighbourhood and friends rather than the generalized requirements of the later stages of formal education. There is no need to sort out strategies for bringing divergent sets of values into line by affecting either the school or the home. The relationship between the two can instead be seen as a dynamic one in which the interactive process is crucial and is likely to be the source of any improvement in home-school relations. 'Community education', as dispensed by schools, usually means parents and their neighbours can use the schools' facilities. Opportunities for members of the community to participate in the control or operation of educational institutions do exist but are isolated.[4] Similarly, the 'community-oriented' curriculum, in its present manifestations, may select its topics from the immediate environment, but rarely selects people from that environment who can contribute to the learning processes. The teacher has yet to be heard who claims he has pupils who are disadvantaged because of lack of contact with the blue-collar population. At the pre-school stage the chances of community participation in education in both of the above senses are at their greatest. The intellectual development of the very young is still largely in the hands of the family, peers and neighbourhood. At later stages education will fall increasingly into the hands of the professional, but during the hand-over period there is ample opportunity and reason for the participation of parents and other adults in the more formal aspects of learning. Conversely, the leader of the pre-school group (or whatever alternative arrangement might replace the group in some cases)[5] is in a good position to use the knowledge and abilities possessed by various members of the community, particularly the parents of the children involved, and to ensure that the first formal educational experiences of those children are specific to them and their own cultural backgrounds. The pre-school leader is better placed than the primary school teacher to be responsive to the characteristics and needs of intake in this way (but not always) because the pre-school group's organization and methods are likely to be more fluid than those of the school, where there are more strict restraints upon the curriculum: children are expected to read and write within a year or two of joining school, and if other objectives are substituted they tend to be regarded by parents and other teachers as merely progressive and as hindering children's competitive chances in educational selection. People who work with the under-fives will also find it easier than many school-based professionals to make contact with the community in which they work by the expedient of including the child's whole family and neighbourhood within the framework of their activities, perhaps even as partners in those activities, since they already possess a mutual independent concern over the child's development. Here, then, are two good reasons why it is feasible as well as necessary for some form of joint participation between supplier and consumer to occur. The academic arguments about the emphases of early education need now to be extended to include the question of strategies by which the various coinages of infant education are being minted and circulated into wider currency.

Intervention strategies

Strategies designed to deal with the misalignment of schools' and families' values are inevitably concentrated in the pre-school and infant years. It is at this time that parents and school share most equally the tasks of socializing the child; and it is at this time that the greatest opportunity exists for co-operation in those tasks between the family and the nursery or school, both because of the still considerable influence of parents in the child's development at that stage and because the formal agencies are under the least pressure from academic requirements.

Although there are other stages at which deliberate intervention in education and development can be undertaken profitably on an experimental basis, the years of early infancy seem to be crucial and to offer the possibility of a wide application of methods suited to children of all types of ability and origin.

Pre-schooling is only one critical stage, but one which can be, and is being, managed on a large scale at present. The fact that joining school represents a crisis of continuity to the young child, especially one who has not been bred into the schools' value systems, requires that the development of pre-school provision and its links with infant school be specifically geared to that young child. Part 2 of this volume proposes ways in which it is possible for pre-school groups to adopt the necessary individualistic and diagnostic approach toward the child and family while retaining an awareness among teachers of the cultural contexts in which they were working. A number of promising lines of work in this field are in progress in Britain, ranging from small-scale demonstrations to medium-scale projects. Some are quite similar to the approach proposed here. Others adopt what we have called a unilateralist approach, and concentrate mainly on the reinforcement of traditional school objectives for all infants; these programmes also have their strengths, not least of which is that they tend to be more immediately applicable to existing nurseries and infant schools. Such is free enterprise in ideas and action that many approaches should be tried. All, however, face the problem of implementation; again, such is the free market that each will win a portion of it by force of its feasibility, appeal, and publicity in the right quarters. To varying extents the take-up of a programme or approach may also depend upon supporting research.

Early education programmes

Strategies, as discussed here, imply change, but change occurs and will continue to occur in the approach adopted by teachers and families toward the education of the young without any conscious strategy being evolved. When the change is more consciously and deliberately sought, however, greater or lesser degrees of design are involved in the process. The field of early education has developed, in advance of other areas of social engineering, a peculiar form of planned, or controlled, intervention. An early form of controlled intervention was known as curriculum development, a process in which new ideas based, soundly or unsoundly, on prior learning theory, were built into a curriculum which was implemented on a small-scale basis and monitored in order to observe its effectiveness and sometimes to suggest modifications. In a more general form this process has been applied beyond curricula to whole programmes, which may contain curricular elements. This model, known as action-research in Britain, has been applied most extensively and earliest in the USA, and only quite recently in Britain and other parts of Europe. Its scientific heritage is the methodology of experimentation and it has been fostered by the demand for special programmes, in particular for underachievers. Perhaps in the absence of clear guides for action from survey-type research, the methodology of limited experimentation has become a major tool of investigation in the study of educational disadvantage. Experimentation has its drawbacks, too. Key variables such as teacher personality and individual child characteristics will be under-represented in small-scale try-outs, so that results will be generalizable to a wider population only in part. Often, too, special programmes contain a greater investment of resources and expertise than would be possible in a large-scale replication. Hodges,[6] on the other hand, designed a programme without an intensive input of personnel and resources, excluding also parents' participation in the programme, just so that it could be implemented more readily in existing schools. Special programmes cannot easily take into account the cultural antecedents of underachievement: many programmes in the USA have attempted to compensate for deprivation by educational means, by selecting their clientele from the poor, but little information is available about the operation of the programme with other groups. Other programmes have used low intelligence test scores as criteria for inclusion regardless of cultural factors or of higher IQ groups, so that it is again difficult to define the population for which the programme works, if it does. Compensatory pre-school programmes, particularly the earlier examples developed in the USA, and their derivatives, have often proceeded by rejecting rather than respecting the child's development up to that point in some way. Sometimes the child was physically removed from his usual environment, to summer camps or integrated schools, for instance; at other times intensive instruction in the deficient skills was attempted. Since the Head Start programme in the USA increasingly sophisticated approaches have been developed from that original experience. Many of them have been encouraging, and some of these are discussed in other chapters. The notion of compensation is retained by many programme organizers, however, who either ignore the parents' possible contributions to their children's development by following a strictly cognitive content, or try to influence the parents in their own professional image.

Specifically developed programmes in Britain are relatively few at present. No doubt this paucity reflects the low priority given to experimentation in general, and the consequently meagre funds it attracts, but it is also a function of the rather different political aspect of educational innovation in Britain. In the USA and many European nations where action-research projects have been conducted, there is a real possibility that a well tried method will be taken up on a large scale, perhaps by whole states. In the less centralized British educational system, however, an innovation succeeds on its own merits or propaganda and its appeal to individual teachers and officials. The British context encourages a diversity of exploration and experiment, but it is also more commercially competitive and often the crudest and simplest panaceas sell best, particularly when it is a question of producing equipment for the less sceptical or achievement-oriented parents. There are nevertheless a number of British action-research projects with an academic rather than commercial basis, which should be mentioned, despite their limited generality, for they highlight the difficulties of recommending policies by this method.

The British reaction to the development of compensatory strategies for infants consists in a diversity of localized provisions, reported in Chapter 6, and four major research projects. When the National Foundation for Educational Research launched its Compensatory Education project (later called the Pre-school Education project) it became the first British programme to introduce and evaluate pre-school intervention. It used a highly structured programme (the Peabody Language Development Kit) given for short daily periods by project staff to the children of local nursery classes. Various other strategies, such as weekly meetings of mothers, have also been tried, but no quantitative results of the main intervention are to hand at the time of writing. By selecting whole classes in 'light grey' areas the project was not confined to children from low economic status homes or with a narrow range of ability. The project made some attempt, however, to select nursery classes with children 'at educational risk', and the main objective was to combat that risk with a cognitive, structured programme.

The Schools Council's research project in compensatory education,[7] operated along different lines, in concentrating on providing methods and materials for teachers and officials who were concerned in the development of the child, particularly the deprived child. Four lines of approach were adopted, the first of which was the prediction of performance at school by reference to child and home-related variables. This prediction exercise was undertaken in order to provide a screening process for use in identifying children, rather than areas, in need of additional educational attention. Second, a more detailed study was carried out of the dynamic processes operating between the homes of deprived children and their development at the infant school stage, in order to understand the effects of material and cultural deprivation. Third, materials and programmes were produced which were aimed especially at improving educational development of deprived children; and fourth, since the project was based in Swansea, the particular effects were studied of deprivation upon Welsh-speaking children who have the problem of learning English as a second language.

A further Schools Council project is in progress which also falls within the concept of the monitored development of pre-school and infant strategies. It is known as the Schools Council Project on Communication Skills in Early Childhood, it runs until 1976 and is an attempt to provide methods and materials which will assist teachers in handling the development of linguistic skills in young infants. While not designed explicitly for disadvantaged children, the work does originate from a prior longitudinal study of language development which identified, as Bernstein's studies have, different uses and styles of language among different social groups. The project proceeds, in fact, by not identifying disadvantaged children, but in the expectation that they will benefit particularly. While fostering an appreciation in teachers of different styles of communication among children, it is not yet clear what kind of strategy is to be recommended: whether, in taking account of styles which are not consistent with the usual media of school learning, teachers will be able to use and extend those styles or will seek to standardize them—these two goals, on the other hand, may each be appropriate at different stages.

The National EPA Experiment,[8] sponsored by the Department of Education and Science and the Social Science Research Council, was an attempt to develop strategies which would improve the educational environment in educational priority areas. Separate action-research teams were set up in five varied educational priority areas to pursue their own solutions to the areas' problems. The solutions which were tried out and evaluated ranged over a wide area of social action; in three of the areas, in Liverpool, Birmingham and the West Riding of Yorkshire, a common pre-school programme was pursued and centrally evaluated. In this experiment the Peabody Language Development Kit was, as in the NFER project, used in normal nursery classes.

The West Riding team, during the project and afterwards, used pre-school intervention as a major strategy. The main reasons for pre-school featuring predominantly in the EPA experiment were the accumulating empirical evidence that experience during the early years of childhood was a crucial determinant of later psychological development, and the increasing volume of information on pre-school programmes from the USA. It was thought that intervention at the pre-school stage could be one of the keys to the educational problems of the type of area under study. It is important to place this strategy in the context which A.H. Halsey, the director of the national EPA experiment, has elaborated in *Educational Priority*, vol. 1. Pre-school intervention can be only one of the keys, others being family, school and local social structure, but one which is more amenable to direct change, being relatively undeveloped, and one which links those other influences together through its concern with socialization at an important juncture in the child's career.

Readers may feel that there are important developments in pre-school strategies other than the four listed here; indeed there are, and many of them are discussed in other chapters, particularly in Chapters 4 and 6. The purpose in this chapter, rather, is to examine the idea of the monitored development which may provide bases for action on a wider front, if conditions are favourable, and to see what difficulties lie in the way of this deliberate, researched form of innovation. There is also the requirement that the projects relate at least to the pre-school years, although most extend beyond also. In considering the EPA experiment, many promising lines of development outside the pre-school sector were not mentioned; the home-visiting approach is covered elsewhere in this volume and readers interested in the project's other developments are referred to the sources already quoted, and to those volumes of *Educational Priority* which have appeared since vol. 1, dealing with each area's activities in turn. The remainder of this chapter is given over to considering a number of topics which arise when change, especially project-initiated change, is proposed in the early education sector.

Unilateral versus co-operative approaches

Policies for acclimatizing children to formal education, it has been implied earlier, may be directed toward bringing nurseries or schools' expectations of children into line with the families they serve, or families' expectations into line with the more formal demands of the educational institutions. Occasionally, as in the passage quoted earlier from *Educational Priority*, vol. 1, simultaneous change in both is advocated so that some kind of meeting on central, if not neutral, ground may occur. Even more occasional is the suggestion that home and school may co-operate to work out a mutually satisfying approach in a practical setting. It is not difficult to understand why co-operation is so rare within the school system: such a style of community-oriented or family-based learning involves a good deal of upheaval in the structures of most schools. In the pre-school field there would appear to be few such obstacles to a co-operative approach, yet even at the level of the small-scale demonstration project or experimental pre-school there are certain less tangible resistances to its development.

There is a manifest problem in promoting strategies which will lead to co-operation between the several parties to socialization, in that they are not easily devised, implemented and evaluated. The unilateral programme, particularly the kit or curriculum directed at the class or nursery is recognizable as an educational technique and is acceptable to professionals in the field. It is easy to see also why unilateral strategies are concentrated in the school or pre-school context rather than the home context. The agencies exist in the formal system which can act as media for change, although they will often act to resist changes. In most communities, however, there are no similar mediating institutions.

There are problems also in demonstrating the value of the programme which is more broadly based than that which accelerates fairly conventional cognitive development. It is extremely difficult to obtain research results which convincingly demonstrate the efficiency of a particular programme or approach. Programmes with limited but intensively pursued aims[9] are capable of producing impressive short-term improvements in measured abilities, while less direct intervention through the manipulation of the mother–child relationship, for instance, will tend to show up less evidently on similar measures, since the input is diffuse compared with the tested outcome. This difficulty is in part no doubt due to the lack of reliable tests capable of measuring the attainment of non-cognitive developmental criteria, and perhaps also to the problems of specifying the objectives of a programme with a more comprehensive approach than the purely cognitive. When it is a question of assessing the long-term effectiveness of various types of programme, the research evidence is again of limited value, since any gain during the programme tends to be lost gradually over the succeeding years whether the programme objectives were exclusively cognitive or not. Again, it may be that the measures are inadequate to pick up actual retained gains in other areas, or that progress stops when intervention stops.

In the absence of clear research evidence on the effectiveness of various types of pre-school intervention, critical appraisal has been directed at the details of the relevant studies in an attempt to isolate factors which might contribute to an effective programme of intervention. Weikart,[10] writing on the articulated series of programmes operated by the High/Scope Foundation since 1960, extracts two points regarding effective pre-schools; these are planning and supervision. By planning, he suggests the organization of the day-to-day activities both in detail and in order to form a sequenced totality; planning offers the opportunity for the adults to integrate themselves and their ideas, for the programme to be paced and for discussions on children's progress and the relation of theory and practice to take place. Good supervision not only complements planning but ensures that it takes place; an effective leader will enable the individual and general difficulties of the group to be aired and resolved.

Bronfenbrenner,[11] taking a rather different approach, examines the experiences of a small number of experiments with pre-school groups and home-visiting approaches. Concluding, with many others, that a short, once-and-for-all programme cannot be expected to produce long-term gains since it can attack only a small part of the wider problem of lack of educational opportunity, he extrapolates a continuous series of possible intervention techniques. The series begins with preparation for parenthood among school children and continues with intervention in families before children arrive, at the time of birth and during the first three years of life at home. Experience at pre-school groups is recommended for the ages four to six and from six to twelve a system of parent support for the child at school is outlined.

A series of interventions such as that suggested by Bronfenbrenner has the encouraging aspect that the impetus given in the early stages is maintained and built upon. The successive stages are practicable within existing systems of family care and school provision in the USA and to some extent in Britain also. Neither is it a completely unilateral approach in that it does recognize the family as an agency in the learning process, but whether as an active one generating its own styles and ends or a passive agency for carrying out procedures devised by professional educators alone is an open question. The format of continuous intervention allows for either a co-operative or an imposed content at any of its stages; the choice depends very much on the attitudes to education and society of the programme initiators.

Each of the British action-research projects cited in this chapter started with the patronage of administrators and professional educators and, at least at first, these projects have been compensatory in that they take the education system's formal experiences as valid aims for infants. To some extent also, since they were concerned at least in part with the educational problems of disadvantaged children, they acknowledge that children's home experiences may not be an appropriate preparation for formal schooling. The Schools Council's compensatory education and communication skills projects adopt a totally unilateral approach since their techniques are designed for use by teachers; it is true that these techniques are intended to encourage teachers to be aware of children's linguistic or social backgrounds, but how much this awareness leads to an explicit inclusion of that background into the learning processes will, as in Bronfenbrenner's model, depend a lot on the practitioner. The NFER and the EPA experiment's pre-school projects, in using language kits were in some ways more rigidly unilateralist (perhaps through the influence of American programmes) but in their later developments began to involve parents at some point in their curricula, the West Riding EPA project's pre-school groups and educational-visitor scheme eventually employing a high degree of parent- and child-initiated content. It is not surprising that the two Schools Council projects, being based in early school, should use school-based techniques while the NFER and EPA projects, working in nurseries, should venture into their catchment areas.

Discrimination for or against?

Most of the projects quoted in this volume address themselves in some fashion to the issue of differing home and school norms. We have tried to argue that how one sees this difference, as a deficiency on the part of one or a conflict between the two, has serious implications for what action one supports. In this argument we have in many ways equated compensatory and unilateral approaches, implying that these do similar injustice to children's home norms. While this is our view, we would wish to admit that a unilateral approach has some virtues and the co-operative point of view some vices. First, however, let us review our reasons, argued in greater detail in Chapter 1, for opposing a bluntly compensatory approach.

The argument has been put forward earlier that, between them, the public debate on disadvantage and news of educational programmes for deprived children, operating chiefly in the USA, have contributed an enormous amount to a compensatory movement in Britain; this movement would, it is claimed, provide enriching experiences for young children in Britain who live in poor material or social circumstances or otherwise risk poor educational progress. An unfortunate result of this emphasis on domestic and social circumstances and of their conjunction with retardation in school is that they focus attention upon elements in the mismatching of parents' and teachers' expectations which may not in themselves be very significant. They may mislead administrators and educators into glibly espousing ineffective or damaging policies. There are two outstanding expressions of this prejudicial view of the abilities of children from poor homes, one at the level of the individual teacher, the other at the level of public administration.

In the case of the individual teacher, one excuse for prejudice against pupils of apparently low potential has given way to another, more sophisticated reason for discriminating. During the 1960s the theory became current, based on several research studies,[12] that teachers' perceptions of a pupil's abilities could influence the development of those abilities, even where the perceptions were irrelevant or false. In so far as these suggestions reached schools they undoubtedly had some effect in inhibiting teachers from making hasty judgments of pupils with runny noses, grubby knees and tatty shirts. More recently, however, much of this inhibition against unfair perceptions of pupils has quite probably evaporated in the heat of the discussion about home backgrounds and the way they might affect performance. The possibility for adverse discrimination against children from materially impoverished homes will not be reduced by labelling the children disadvantaged, with the apparent support of expensive and rigorous research projects. One of the authors found himself in a classroom, not in Britain, confronted by a teacher of six-year-olds who stated: 'You can't expect too much from these children with their backgrounds, they're disadvantaged.'

At the national level, too, unwarranted assumptions about the causes of underachievement have led to the allocation of financial resources unequally, partly according to indicators of social conditions. Educational priority areas are designated according to criteria which vary according to locality but which usually have been shown to associate with low average achievement in the schools; achievement itself is included in the list of indicators used. Indicators which take account of school factors such as space and teacher–pupil ratios are fairly defensible on common sense grounds since these relate to basic resources and they are applied to specific schools, not areas. Those indicators which are based on the easily measurable aspects of children's backgrounds, however, such as average family income or density of housing, are not likely to place extra resources most efficiently where needed, since poor performance is not necessarily the direct product of such factors. This is not to deny that in some, perhaps many, instances the extra allocations made under the EPA programme do incidentally make a difference, but it does suggest that as a strategy positive discrimination by area according to average social indicators is not likely to be productive in the way intended.

If educational resources are scarce, and if the progress of certain children appears to be hindered by non-inherent factors, then there is a strong argument for positive discrimination of some kind (provided, that is, the recipients are not thereby discriminated against, because of any stigma attached to the extra help, more than they are discriminated for). Where the extra help should be placed is not an easy matter to determine. Underachievement is a simple criterion to apply for school-aged children although it has been criticized as an inefficient means of identifying individual underachievers. It is claimed,[13] for instance, that many underachievers exist outside educational priority areas and that not all those within such areas are falling short of their potential. The difficulty with this view is that of isolating children's individual potential: when can low achievement be shown to be due to remediable circumstances within the local context? That is to say, when does low achievement become underachievement? The notion of positive discrimination by area depends heavily on the reliability of average achievements for predicting the presence of local school-based or area-based inhibiting factors. It does not follow that all individuals in the area will be equally subject to the inhibitors, but if differential allocations of resources are to be made there seems no reliable guide other than underachievement, however rigidly school-based such a notion is.

To look beyond actual average school achievements as a guide to distributing extra assistance seems a very dubious policy in the light of our earlier discussion of the relation of the social antecedents of achievement.

In *From Birth to Seven,*[14] the association between birth factors and later physiological development was used, on the whole quite validly, to construct a predictive model for poor development such that individuals who are at risk may be identified early and receive special treatments or observations: the process is known as selective medical screening. To translate this model by analogy to the socio-educational sphere, which is what positive discrimination by area on social criteria does attempt, is largely invalid on two counts. First, selective medical screening is applied to individuals or to groups with similar histories, whereas positive discrimination in education treats groups with average deviant scores on the criteria. Second, the connection between medical factors and physiological development is probably more direct and certainly more intelligible than that between social background factors and educational attainment.

The problems of positive discrimination apply also to the pre-school sphere, at least until nursery expansion fulfils demand. Here, however, there cannot readily be complete screening for educational achievements since the child population does not compulsorily attend an educational establishment where the testing can easily be carried out as part of school routine. In our later comments the implicit requirement for some form of positive discrimination in pre-schooling facilities is borne in mind, but in general the view is taken that the difficulties in matching parents' and teachers' expectations and their abilities to provide beneficial educational experiences for their children can be found in any locality. The difficulties are taken to exist at least as much on the level of specific interactions between family members, the community and the local education system as on the level of generalized sociological theories of disadvantage.

Returning now to our discussion of specifically constructed intervention strategies, and leaving for the moment the wider policy issue of the appropriate levels on which to intervene, or discriminate, we can see more readily why compensation or discrimination can be a misplaced, even dangerous, strategy. If the teacher goes beyond the nursery or classroom walls, however, or admits others within them, other kinds of dangers are risked. It is mentioned elsewhere that the programme based upon an easily assimilable and formal content is generally simpler to implement and evaluate than the programme with more diffuse objectives or than actions with no objectives at all to speak of. The curriculum development project, therefore, is a good investment since the pay-off is recognizable and predictable. Many of the intervention schemes described have relied heavily on language development kits, for instance. Such approaches have little need to concern themselves with children's cultural backgrounds since, it is plausibly argued, the higher reaches of the education system and occupational structure, which are of an inflexible nature, feed on conventional educational attainments and qualifications, not on abilities whose value is mediated by the domestic and community context in which they were reared. In this connection we would oppose this argument only at the point where it assumes that conventional means are necessary at the age of joining school in order to achieve conventional ends in secondary school and later.

The possibility of separating conventional ends from the means of achieving them is also a key to the problem which socially relevant curricula at pre-school or school run into, namely that children on curricula designed for a lower social class will be disadvantaged by them even more than by a conventional curriculum, so that they will be doomed to second-class citizenship. Certainly, if special curricula are promoted for the victims of social or material disadvantage, the result would be at least as divisive as the compensatory strategies for the disadvantaged which we have been criticizing. It is precisely for this reason that the determination of methods by social criteria has been resisted in our argument, and that relevance to the individual has been recommended as the primary force behind educational techniques above relevance to the community or wider society. Where cultural relevance comes in, it will hopefully be made clear in Part 2, is where it determines the starting point for education at the semi-formal pre-school stage, as it does for children of all social origins; it is less appropriate to treat children's cultural milieu either as a means of identifying children or areas in need of special programmes—which is a compensatory point of view—or as an entity to be preserved throughout the child's career to the exclusion of conventional educational values—which is perhaps an extreme extension of a community education approach. It hardly seems likely that a culturally relevant starting point in education will compound the handicap of a child who is already seen as educationally disadvantaged because of adverse social conditions, especially when one considers that the educational disadvantage itself is apparent only to the extent that such children fall behind in the conventional educational races.

Adopting strategies

Before continuing along the obstacle course of problems which surround the implementation of strategies, let us refer to an action-research project, in the Netherlands, which is remarkable in that very few of the moral and technical obstacles with which we are concerned seem to apply. The project in question is a pre-school group in a suburb of Haarlem which houses, mostly in high-rise flats, a population of about 3,000. The building which houses the group was provided by the local education authority which also provides a teacher and enables an educational psychologist and students to offer their services to the group. Probably all the parents of attenders are heavily involved by participating in the group or providing peripheral assistance; they were also responsible for converting and preparing the building and grounds, mainly according to their own requirements. At the time of writing, the group is a much-visited demonstration project which is being continuously evaluated according to cognitive and attitudinal measures being developed for the purpose. So far, the structure of the enterprise is familiar in other projects. The Haarlem group, however, was decided on and set up by the parents, who were dissatisfied with the existing arrangements for their children.[15] What this project provides which others do not, is the example of action-research in which the action was not specifically set up for the purpose of evaluation by professional interventionists. It is also a rare example of a co-operative enterprise originating from the community rather than the educators. The group achieves what action-research teams can rarely do, that is, evaluate a pre-existing development; in the Haarlem project we have a spontaneous development with all its inherent enthusiasm and stumbling-blocks, not set up in the image of its professional makers but in that of its clients. The co-operation which exists between professional and non-professional workers, likewise, has not been imported from a remote theoretical source and implanted in the group but arose from the desire for all participants to assist in the same process of learning and providing mutual support. It is almost certain that the group is no longer what it was at the outset, because of the continuous interest of outsiders; published reports are not available at the time of writing, but will surely be awaited with great interest.

Whether early education strategies include or ignore children's primary, local learning experiences, they are almost inevitably initiated in a unilateral fashion by professional educators, so that with the exception described above, the approach will hardly ever be totally co-operative. Even with strongly community-oriented goals, workers in the field will find themselves in a position of channelling more information from the field towards administrators than in the reverse direction, so that control over the programme and its proliferation lies firmly in the hands of those who are identified with the formal system of education: even the impetus for an ordinary pre-school group with high parent participation will have to come from its leader. So axiomatic is this principle of innovation that it is well to recognize that any strategy discussed here begins with an imposition on either the suppliers or the consumers of educational resources. It must be admitted too that the imposition has to be conducted delicately in order to work, whether it is being made upon fellow-professionals or fellow-members of a community. Many educationists feel that interference in the pre-school sector by making demands on the families of pre-school children is unjustified, and with this point of view we would sympathize a good deal. Others may argue that teachers are already conducting a form of interference in family values on a grand scale by promoting an education which in many cases conflicts with those values. In fact, all education is a form of intervention, and indeed a form of compensation for those children who do not readily accept the styles in which formal learning is conducted. There seems a very great difference to us, however, between an established form of intervention which has become compulsory, as school has, and a service such as pre-school, which is yet developing and is used by parents according to demand. This difference between the school system and pre-school facilities suggests two slightly conflicting views of pre-school innovation. In the first place, a new service or facility generally requires a more thoughtful approach than the administration of an existing service which has a conservative history to back it up and gain acceptance for it. The carefulness with which changes need to be argued for applies *a fortiori* to the pre-school sector, where different approaches are numerous and in competition; to some extent this consideration will also apply in the school sector, for instance in the case of an experimental school or in the case of curricular development. In the second place, however, since pre-school is not compulsory or zoned, parents can take it or leave it; where it is in short supply freedom of choice is limited but still present. This free enterprise situation permits, and appears to encourage, the diversity of approach referred to above. We can find no strong reason for restricting this diversity, particularly if it means that co-operative pre-school enterprises, in which families' and communities' demands can find expression, as well as other models of pre-school provision, are better able to flourish.

Group versus individual approaches

There is a good deal of controversy between educational strategies about what is the appropriate size of unit for intervention in promoting programmes of pre-school education. Some see early education as primarily the identification and encouragement of individual children's abilities and interests, while others stress the character of the area or community in which the project operates as the proper object of study. In the present volume these approaches are discussed, particularly in Chapters 4 and 5 where the individual and community aspects are separated in order to sharpen the analysis of these two bases of learning. Individual tutoring and the Schools Council communication skills project are examples which do not necessarily involve social analysis at all, whereas the EPA pre-school experiment, the Schools Council compensatory education project and the NFER project all required the groups or areas studied to contain children who were low achievers or from impoverished families, in a material or social sense.

It is perhaps obvious from this way of presenting the difference between individual and group approaches that the socially oriented projects may nevertheless use practical techniques (such as individual tutoring) in pursuing their aims, while the individual approach may be applied with or without consideration of the community or group in which it is being used. The controversy will become clearer if we separate the concept of analysing the social bases of learning and learning difficulties from the application of techniques to cope with them. The policy of positive discrimination in educational priority areas may be used to apply a variety of extra resources. As a national policy it is used to allocate additional material and financial assistance to schools situated in areas with educational and social difficulties. In the five-area EPA experiment, whole programmes both individual and area-based were developed with a view to extending them on a basis of positive discrimination; as one could expect, political, economic and methodological problems have prevented such an extension of any of the programmes which were developed, as yet. The Schools Council's compensatory education project worked mainly in the field of social analysis, developing predictive machinery which could be used as a screening procedure for individual families or children. As in the medical analogy, once screening has revealed individuals who are at risk, the 'treatment' will depend upon further diagnosis. Positive discrimination and screening are both methods of allocating scarce resources on the basis of a socio-educational analysis; they do not include a definition of those resources, and may be applied in allocating resources of very different kinds; some resources like compensatory educational programmes, or educational-visiting, or curricula for special schools will perhaps be developed especially for the purpose.

It is the analysis according to which resources are being directed, whether they are directed for instance in an EPA policy or a pre-school expansion policy, which is at the root of the problem of area versus individual intervention. From the attempt to discriminate positively in the EPA projects two rather different approaches to the problem of analysing the need for additional resources emerged. Two members of the ILEA research and statistics group have claimed[16] that the designation of educational priority areas was inefficient in the context in which they were operating. Almost as many children were to be found outside as in EPA schools who were at risk according to the indices on which educational priority areas were designated. Furthermore, in EPA schools those not considered at risk outnumbered those who were. Gaps were discovered in average performance between those who were considered at risk and those who were not, regardless of school attended. The at-risk group in EPA schools averaged three months of reading age behind a similarly defined group in more privileged schools, but the average achievement of the sector not at risk also appeared to suffer from attendance at schools in problem areas. This mere selection of findings, taken out of the full context of the paper, are intended to show that the concepts of social disadvantage, poor achievement and an adverse school environment can be separated empirically to a quite large extent and that there is a certain overlap in the range of achievement between one type of school and another and one type of family or child and another. Suggestions such as these will strengthen both the case for individual attention to children's learning difficulties, with some attention given to inhibiting family and material circumstances by means of screening, and the case for additional help for schools in difficulties, perhaps according to quite separate screening procedures.

In the West Riding EPA project's pre-school programme, both during the period of the national EPA experiment and afterwards, when the hybrid group became more highly developed, a quite different approach to positive discrimination was taken. Here, almost implicitly, designation as an educational priority area was taken as an indication of a series of educational and social problems which assailed the whole town. The limited intervention of pre-school provision was therefore supplemented by strategies aimed at social problems, such as including a social worker on the team and making residential provision for children in times of family crisis. In developing those strategies it has to be appreciated that disadvantage in relation to educational opportunity was only one of the problems assailing the project areas. Along with reduced economic and social opportunity it presents a formidable barrier to individual and collective development. Such an analysis, as in the reports of many compensatory studies, naturally places severe limitations on the value of the experimental findings in implementing direct improvements in the educational and other opportunities available in areas of deprivation. Pre-school and similar strategies are therefore incomplete solutions to the problems which the national EPA experiment, for instance, was set. It cannot be concluded, however, that they are irrelevant to those problems. The fact that comprehensive solutions do not exist as yet is not a reason for refraining from ameliorative strategies entirely if they are believed to be effective within their proper sphere of influence. Other aspects of reduced opportunities are being tackled by other experiments in educational and social policy, such as those conducted under Urban Aid Grants and by the Community Development Projects. Some of these experiments are designed to refine other elements of the general strategy for situational and structural change. It was indeed the West Riding EPA project's experience that the sources of the lack of educational opportunity were located in a wider context than the purely educational, and that an individualistic approach alone would not be adequate as a continuing strategy. As a result of this interrelation between inhibiting elements in the local society, positive discrimination on an area basis seemed an essential part of the required approach, but one which should be complemented by developments in that community on the social and economic fronts also.

The conflict between these two studies in positive discrimination is partly explained by the social and educational contexts in which they were made. Whereas the West Riding town was one of relatively homogeneous composition, in demographic terms. Inner London is certainly not. In educational terms alone, an area, or even a school-based designation of need is unlikely to be strategically appropriate where average achievements between schools vary as much as they do in Inner London; in the West Riding project area the differences in average achievements between infant schools were very slight. Incidentally, only half the schools in the town were officially designated EPA, showing that the more broadly based criteria for designation can discriminate where educational criteria alone may not.

Discrimination in favour of schools, groups, or areas seems to run certain risks in implementation, on whichever basis it is carried out; where pre-school places or purpose-built schools, for instance, are in short supply the arguments for distributing them according to need are, however, very strong. A policy of screening so that pre-school places, or special attention in school classes, can be administered individually will run the risk that the individuals become stigmatized in the eyes of peers, families and teachers; it is very difficult however strong the intention, for a teacher to avoid using the knowledge that a child has been singled out for attention, perhaps on social grounds, in a way which will prejudice that child's development but this difficulty is hardly greater than that of using individual records transmitted from one school or class to another. Areas, too, may be stigmatized. The West Riding project area received adverse publicity in local and national press, and on television, which jeopardized the project's work considerably because the town's population felt it had been isolated for special attention. Teachers in EPA schools often feel that designation is an adverse judgment on their schools rather than a means of assistance in the face of unusual difficulties; many teachers would prefer to forgo the assistance in order to avoid the stigma.

In considering alternative bases or units of intervention, we have the situation that both the institutional and the individual level are possible depending on the context, and that each has its practical difficulties. A too explicit imposition of discriminatory methods is likely to stigmatize and perhaps to encourage unjust expectations. If either is based on an analysis of disadvantage which includes social indicators, these practical dangers are greater because the expectations may be based on assumptions about the influence of social background on ability which are too strong.

Pre-school expansion is a field in which these arguments apply strongly. Whereas any intervention in the primary school system and beyond has necessarily to be conducted at the institutional level (except, perhaps, when individuals are collected together in special classes), pre-school provision may be provided on an individual or area basis. *A Framework for Expansion,*[17] recognizing that pre-school places will be in short supply in the initial stages of expansion, proposes that local education authorities have regard to areas and sectors of particular need with a view to concentrating provision there first. Need clearly implies social deprivation, for former Urban Aid criteria, similar to EPA criteria, are suggested for identifying areas of need within local education authorities, and this is a direct form of positive discrimination. In offering children places, nursery teachers or pre-school leaders, if they are not operating a waiting list on a strictly 'first-come, first served' basis, are operating an informal type of screening, often based on families' circumstances. Within the existing and the expanding system of pre-school provision, therefore, a process of individual selection, if not individualized attention, is being conducted, often on social grounds. In other instances, any notion of prior needs is discounted, or even reversed by admitting first those whose parents have been provident enough to place their children on one or more waiting lists. The placing of pre-school groups again determines the extent to which need or demand are met. Here, a free enterprise system of private development tends to favour sectors with a high, or vociferous, demand but low relative need if need is determined according to the material and educational environments. An expanding state system will tend to avoid the low need areas while nursery units are so thin on the ground where those in need live. It is to understanding and anticipating these processes of expansion, these expressions of need and demand for pre-school education, and the various techniques for providing the service that the arguments of the foregoing and following chapters are addressed.

Suggestions as to the ways in which a co-operative approach to early education might be achieved are made in Part 2 of this volume. In those chapters, appropriate strategies at the pre-school and infant school levels are considered, together with the difficulties of implementing these and other methods of innovation.

Part 2

Pre-school and the community

3

A case study: the Red House pre-school groups

John is three years old. He sits on a heap of derelict rubble throwing pieces of brick at a battered dustbin. His friends join in the game until one of them hits John with a brick. A chase begins over the rubble, up a steep bank along a narrow-edged wall until John traps his assailant and thumps him. Both children run home where a neighbour friend of John's mother tells them to be quiet, gives them sweets and sends them outside once more to play. The two boys find a puddle of rain water in the street and commence to tread carefully around the edge, looking into their reflections in the water, without speaking. Suddenly John stamps into the puddle drenching his companion. 'You bugger.' A chase ensues.

Elaine is also three. She sits in a play house which is part of the equipment installed in a new nursery unit. Three other children wander into the play house, take toy cups and saucers from a cupboard and set them out on a low table. They sit around the table and one of the children pours imaginary tea into their cups. Elaine pushes the cups on the floor saying that the table is her pastry board and that she is about to do some baking. An argument commences over the use of the table. A nursery assistant enters the play house and sits at the table to talk to the children. 'I was here first', says Elaine. 'We had the table.' Eventually the assistant fetches dough and the whole group cut out jam tarts on the table. This is followed by a tea party held by the four children. The nursery assistant leaves them and the children continue role-playing as mother and father of two children. After a few minutes Elaine moves away to a book corner and sits by herself where she remains unnoticed.

Robert is the same age as John and Elaine. He sits with his mother and a teacher playing a game with bricks. They build a tower together on the floor. 'Let's make it higher.' The teacher adds a brick. 'Now you make the tower higher.' Robert adds another brick. His mother builds another tower. 'Is this tower as high as yours, Robert?' The teacher moves away to another group activity in which another mother paints with three children. 'Tell me about your pictures.' The painters describe their paintings and the mother in the group carries on the conversation while the teacher moves to another group. Nine adults and twenty-five children are in the room. It is difficult to identify the teacher in the group.

John's case represents a situation which is seen to require compensatory action by some educationists. There is a high probability that John's use of language will be different from that of a child of a similar age living in a more affluent area whose parents' linguistic skills are highly developed. His social skills will differ from children in other areas and his ability to adapt to a school regime requiring closely defined behavioural standards will take longer. John's skill development may be such that his motor skills are well developed while his fine motor skills are underdeveloped. His perceptual skills of sight, touch, hearing are keenly developed but his ability to conceptualize is low. He can communicate his intentions and ideas effectively to his peer group and parents but would find difficulty in communicating in a more elaborated way to peer groups in other areas. He will take longer to adapt to a rigorous school programme aimed at raising his ability to conceptualize and to crack codes of communication.

Elaine has a similar developmental rate both physically and intellectually. She lives in similar home conditions which do not encourage a rapid growth in formal linguistic or conceptual facility. Elaine however has a place in a nursery unit which provides her with the care and concern of a nursery teacher and nursery assistant. For five half-days each week during school terms, she spends her time in a planned environment which has creative materials, exciting apparatus, toys, games and books. Her mother can leave her each morning at the unit knowing that Elaine will be safe, cared for and encouraged to develop social and educational skills which will be valuable during the coming years in full-time school. She knows that Elaine will be encouraged to play, discover and fantasize, to create paintings and models, to listen to stories. She knows, because the nursery teacher has told her so and she has seen the strange paintings brought home on occasions by her daughter. Elaine's mother has a very deep sense of respect for the teacher who is clearly a trained person who knows what is best for Elaine's development. She does not see the nursery unit as a form of compensation for her own inadequacies as a mother but does see the unit as a positive place for her daughter's development. It also allows her to carry out a part-time cleaning job in a nearby store and she need not worry about Elaine getting into mischief. If asked, she would be able to report few details of her child's experience in the nursery unit.

Robert's mother received a visit from the nursery teacher three months before he joined his group. The teacher invited Robert to come to the group to see the nursery and to bring his mother and father. During this evening visit the teacher explained the urgent need for Robert's mother to be with him during nursery sessions. She described the tripartite learning situation which she hoped would develop in the group during the coming year. The parents and teacher would be partners involved in Robert's development. They would meet other mothers and fathers during the year and would be able to see at first hand the important part they were playing in Robert's intellectual development. They would be encouraged to work with Robert in the group and at home. The teacher would also show them how to work with other children in the group. Robert's parents said that they were willing to take part in the nursery group activities and would bring Robert on the commencing date. Their reaction to the invitation was diffident but the teacher's approach to them appeared to offer them equal status with the teacher and they had not previously thought that school normally created this feeling. As the year progressed Robert's mother visited the group each week and stayed for whole sessions. Initially she played with the materials available–sand, clay, water, salt and paint. She learned the vocabulary which springs naturally from the use of such materials and encouraged Robert to use the new words in sentences. The teacher helped her to extend her ability to work with two or three other children and she began to see the differential rate of development in the children within the group. Not all children responded in the same way and at the same pace. She was shown how to develop new sensory and perceptual skills in young children, first individually with Robert, herself and the teacher working away from the main group, later with other children within the group. She understood the reason for colour-matching games, jigsaws, the 'feely' box, bricks and kits which encourage spatial concepts, etc., and soon, Robert's mother became less diffident and, as her confidence grew, it appeared to be transmitted to her son. She was playing a major part in his development not only in 'school' but at home. She bought books, used materials in the evenings, during weekends and holidays just as she had learnt in the group.

Every month the parents held an informal discussion evening in one of their homes with the teacher present. They expressed anxieties about their children, schools, housing, pollution, work but at the same time gained group support as they found common problems and some solutions. More importantly, the group's confidence and morale was high so that they felt able to discuss with teachers in schools points which concerned them about the development of their children. The teacher in the nursery group had created a situation which enabled the potential of the parents to be used effectively with their own children. Such a strategy is very different from one which offers children an enriched situation to compensate for the inadequacies of their parents in developing intellectual and social skills in their children.

The Red House pre-school groups

The group of parents who came regularly to Robert's nursery class are not a fictional collection of adults. The experiences of the pre-school groups held at Red House Centre from 1970 onwards, have provided a wealth of examples which show the positive and negative sides of a strategy recognizing the potential of parents as educators. Such a strategy assumes, of course, that the parents are free to come to the nursery with their children, regularly. Many areas have a high rate of female employment and include a proportion of young mothers in the work force. The pressure to obtain part-time or full-time employment is considerable, especially in urban areas where rents are high, living conditions poor and surroundings desolate. In such areas as many as 40 per cent of mothers may be working on a part-time or full-time basis even when their children are very young. A discussion of alternative types of pre-school provision forms part of Chapter 6 in this book; however, in recognizing the varying problems of areas according to their social or economic make-up, our point is that there are many communities where the majority of parents will be free to spend time with their children on a fairly regular basis.

The pattern which developed in the operation of pre-school groups at Red House commenced with a personal invitation, by the teacher in charge, to families which contained a child of a certain age, living in a particular catchment area. By visiting the homes of these children during evenings preceding the commencement of the school year, she usually met not only the child concerned and its mother but also the father and other siblings. Her invitation was made first to the child, then to the parents who, from the moment of meeting, were recognized as future partners, with the teacher, in helping their child's intellectual social, emotional and physical development and growth. In each case the child was invited to bring his parents to see the Centre which he would be using with other children. A time would be arranged for him to see the current year-group at work and for his parents to meet their parents' group.

Each year approximately twenty-five families were visited in this way. Sometimes two or three calls were made to homes where one or both of the parents were out at the time of the initial visit. The thorough and sensitive way in which these visits were made requires emphasis. Without such an initial approach, which enabled a child to see a stranger called 'a teacher', while he was in the security of his own home, much of the positive, warm response from the families would have been lost. The acceptance of the initial invitation by children and parents was extremely high, enabling the entire age group living within a given catchment area to enter full-time school after a year's pre-school experience in a group. The drop-out rate during each year was low—during a three-year period of operation only two families left the groups.

The year commenced with a complete new intake of children who came accompanied by mothers, or grandmothers, and one or two fathers. Many of the parents knew each other and a few of the children were used to playing together but none of them had been brought together in such a heterogeneous group before. For the first week the parents came with their children and stayed for the complete session. New relationships were being formed within the group but they were also coming to terms with the meaning of their initial invitation to form a partnership with the teacher in the group. There were materials to use and experiment with—many mothers had never played with clay or painted using pots of acrylic or poster paint on large sheets of paper. They saw sand and salt being used to stimulate play, they watched their children explore a new environment in the company of other children of the same age. They began to exchange experiences of child-rearing, stimulated by what they were seeing. The process of learning by the adults from the group had commenced.

Much of the first term was devoted to exploring the use of materials. As the parents played with the materials, the teacher explained the way in which language could be built around an experience. The teacher described the processes of painting, of work with clay, of construction kits, of the play house, in terms of child development. She used the initial stimulus which the parents received from their new experience in creative play to show them the same process of exploration occurring, at a different rate, with their children. The words which could be woven through their explorations were of fundamental importance to the child's intellectual development, in which language adds a new dimension to his thought-processes as well as enabling him to communicate effectively and easily to adults and to other children. She illustrated the young child's need to develop a sense of identity by using examples of individuals adjusting to the group, which at times accepted or at other times rejected them. The teacher was able to construct a two-tier learning system in which she taught the children through the parents.

As the year progressed, skills of cognition and language were introduced to children individually. If a child had difficulty in identifying certain colours, in matching shapes or in recognizing sounds, for example, the teacher provided regular periods when individual teaching was carried out, usually with the parent present. The activities in the individual sessions were compatible with activities carried out in the group, but they provided an accurate record of each child's ability while showing his parents areas of skills which they could help develop. Such individual work could only be carried out because the group of parents and children had bonded well and with two excellent nursery assistants could function effectively without supervision from the teacher.

So the chain reaction of the group development produced a strong, cohesive and purposeful organization which was confident and self-sustaining. During the third and final term some parents were working regularly with small groups of children while others stayed with the group less frequently. The teacher visited the homes of most children each month, particularly those where both parents were working, in order to discuss the child's development and to encourage the parents. Groups of parents met for evening discussion sessions several times each term, either in their homes or in the Centre. The teacher was usually present during these meetings but her role was participant, rather than leading. The discussions helped to develop the confidence of the parents but they were also useful in providing support for individuals who possessed a particular social need. Throughout the year the teacher imparted to the parents her belief in their potential as educators and her conviction that their attitudes were vitally important in the development of their children.

During a typical day in the life of the group the children would be collected by bus at 1 p.m. from pick-up points near their homes. A group of mothers accompany the children. They have arranged between themselves that each day at least four mothers will be present on the bus to supervise the journey. The bus unloads at Red House having completed its first journey of about two miles and will return at 3.30 p.m. to collect the group. The children are greeted by the two nursery assistants as they leave the bus to move inside the building. Children are encouraged to undo their buttons and fastenings, and coats are hung on pegs marked with symbols depicting animals, birds, etc.

The building is quite small. It was previously the family home of a doctor, and it has been modified to provide a multi-purpose room, used by the pre-school group as well as many other groups.[1] The hall, office (quiet room), dining room, workshop and kitchen, are also available for use by the children and their parents, if necessary. Outside there is a large walled garden containing areas of grass, tarmac and trees. The children can play quite safely within the garden and, weather permitting, use its facilities a great deal. On the day being described, an oppresive mist hangs over the valley and trees drip steadily with soot-laden globules of water.

The children move into the multi-purpose room and sit on a rug by the teacher. Parents, nursery assistants and pupils from the local high school also sit down, but on small chairs arranged near the children. The room has been prepared with furniture for three-year-olds to use. The low tables are set in twos and have construction kits, clay, painting materials laid out on them. A play corner is screened off to accommodate toy kitchen furniture, a bed and various utensils. Large building blocks are lying beside an agility mat on the floor while in another corner book-racks made of Tri-wall surround a small square of carpet. Trays of water, sand and salt occupy a further section of floor area.

The teacher welcomes the group to the afternoon session and commences to ask the children about their experiences since they last met on the previous day. They talk about the weather, brothers and sisters (one boy has come with his mother and baby brother today),[2] birthdays, clothes and the usual range of topics explored by teachers and children in nursery or infant groups. The parents form an audience during the conversation and can thus observe the different responses of individuals within the group.

A colour display is being made and the teacher draws attention to the colour being used. One child has brought an old brown shoe, another says that his dad drinks beer from brown bottles. The shoe is added to the display, which is the work of one of the nursery assistants, and the children go to areas of activity which they have chosen. Parents are sitting in most of the areas and join in the activities of building, making, hammering, painting. One is operating a feely box[3] and is encouraging a child to guess the objects and describe their surfaces as 'hard' or 'soft'. Another watches while a group of children build a castle with a table, a blanket and some blocks. Another parent paints, watched by two children who eventually pick up brushes, mix a colour and work on a picture each. When they have finished the parent asks them to tell her what they have painted and she makes a small label to caption each picture.

The room bustles with activity but, strangely, seems to accommodate twenty-five children and ten adults without difficulty. It is hard to identify the teacher or the assistants in the group. In fact, the teacher is not in the room at all. She is sitting in the hall outside the playroom with one child and his mother. Together they are examining a booklet which contains a series of exercises[4] to help motor skill development. A page of the booklet is opened for the child and he is introduced to the exercise by the teacher. As he becomes engrossed in his task the teacher discusses the aims of the exercise with the mother and points out dangers of pressurizing the child to complete the exercises. The mother continues to work with the child while the teacher returns to the playroom to sit in on another activity and work with the parent, this time a father who has returned from a shift in the pit, and with the children.

Later the children are each given a bottle of milk and the adults gather for a cup of tea, when they have an opportunity to discuss the day's work, domestic problems, etc. After their break for milk, some children listen to a story told by one assistant, others sing songs. Since the children are now in other rooms, the business of sorting and mounting paintings can be carried out. Furniture can also be stored away leaving the room ready for cleaning and the next group[5] to use during the evening. After their final session of the afternoon, the children put on coats and hats, helped by all adults present and walk out to the waiting bus. They return home once more escorted by the parents.[6]

The teacher and her two assistants plan the following day's activities in a seminar session with the high school students who have taken part during the afternoon. The behaviour patterns of particular children are discussed in some detail and observations on the way the adults and children interacted are made by the teacher.

The content of each day's activities varied perceptibly but there was a general trend throughout the year to move from exploratory adventures using different materials towards ways of communicating experiences. Play and fantasy were very important elements in the year's work both for the children and the adults. It was possible to use the group to demonstrate the need a child has to play in order to establish his or her identity. The importance of allowing children to play without interference was a harder lesson for adults to learn. It usually required the adults to re-create, through play with paint or clay, the experiences of their childhood before the full realization of this lesson was apparent.

The delicate balance between encouraging play by individuals and groups on the one hand and introducing a form of structure which allows the teacher to identify the skill levels of children on the other hand, requires clear vision by the leader of the group. Play often generated ideas which could be translated into pictures and words later. The visit made by the local fire service at the invitation of the teacher gave rise to spontaneous play by a group of boys in the days following.

The language of the children developed quickly during the year, mainly because of parental stimulus, and displays in the room began to be accompanied by descriptive labels. Books were always available in the room but as their cognitive skills grew, the children began to connect symbolic shapes with sounds. The pre-reading exercises carried out during individual sessions led naturally to children asking to read. A number of the children were reading sentences at the end of the year as a result of being in an environment which included a natural, continuous use of the written and spoken word, not only within the group at the Centre but also in their homes. Books were available from the group's library and also from the local branch of the County library, the staff of which encouraged the parent and children group to use its premises. Toys and books were also sold on market days from the Centre's stall which operated throughout the year. In addition, a local shopkeeper became a stockist for toys, materials and equipment which otherwise were not locally available.

The system supporting the development of each child in the group therefore could be summarized as a pyramid with a number of levels. The first, and nearest to the apex (the child), is formed by the parents, siblings and teacher. At the second level the group of other parents and their children form a supporting, learning agency. The third level contains local resources brought in for young children particularly, in the form of books, toys, materials and equipment which families can buy or borrow. The fourth and lowest level is formed by a community which accepts pre-school experience as desirable for young children and creates an attitude which suggests that pre-schooling is normal when parents and children are working together in a group.

Families and pre-school groups

The origins of the case study described in the previous section are to be found in the research of the 1950s which showed the beneficial effects of early stimulation both in animals and humans. Hunt[7] developed a thesis on the implications of this research for education in early childhood and Bloom's work on the predictive power of IQ scores obtained by five years of age,[8] provided additional support for his thesis.

The pre-school experiment, which formed part of the National Educational Priority Area Project, was based on the assumption that children, whose intellectual development was depressed by environmental and social conditions, would achieve a higher performance in linguistic and cognitive skills if schooling commenced earlier. The West Riding experiment commenced with a group of three-year-olds, who represented most of the intake of a reception class in a local infant school. The first two groups in 1969 had a very limited involvement by parents—the Project's concern was to demonstrate the willingness of parents to allow their children to participate in the programme and to carry out an evaluation of the effects of particular language development schemes.[9]

Follow-up testing has been carried out with these groups in infant and junior schools to the summer of 1973, providing a four-year study of the intellectual development of the children. This has suggested, in common with many studies in the USA, that the objective of cognitive acceleration can be reached with appropriate content and staffing, but cannot be maintained without continued intervention at later stages. Such findings leave open the possibility of unevaluated non-cognitive objectives in the programmes which in a more holistic and continuous approach would be more explicit.

An immediate result of the first pre-school group in 1969 was that an apparent lack of development in manipulative and verbal skills was noted with the intake of three-year-olds. This led to the setting up of a home-visiting scheme (now called 'educational-visiting') in order to work with children aged eighteen to twenty-four months and their parents.

The development of the idea, that parents could form an educational partnership with the teacher both in group work and in home-based work, evolved into a realistic and operational strategy by 1972 at Red House. Unfortunately the funding of the evaluation of the programmes has not permitted a longitudinal study to be made of these more sophisticated developments. We have to rely upon the subjective impressions of the parents, children and teachers taking part.

The most important impact of the later programmes was that they raised the expectations of the parents towards the outcomes of schooling. They had seen their children developing skills in the group and in the visiting sessions which they could identify as helpful during the next year at school. The children were generally happy attending the daily group sessions and looked forward to attending the infant school. The teachers in the two schemes saw considerable gains in the social, emotional and intellectual responses of the children, which was largely due to the interest and involvement of their parents.

The full implication of these outcomes was not realized at the time by the receiving schools. Some children were 'promoted' immediately beyond the reception class, others found the expectations of the teachers lower than in the pre-school group and became bored by the activities offered to them. The adult-child ratio became much lower—a teacher, and possibly an aide, to twenty or thirty children. The regime of parent-teacher partnership in the classroom was over.

The schools had well-established and valid reasons for operating in this way. They were concerned with the well-being of children in their care and not of the well-being of the parents. Indeed, they saw their function, at times, as compensating for the moral and social inadequacies of parents.

This should not be seen as a criticism of the schools involved, if anything it is a criticism of the project for not making the pre-school objectives clearer to school-staffs. It does, however, comment on the watershed which appears to exist in a child's life at the age of five in Britain. It is a watershed which raises at least the following fundamental issues for pre-school activities.

1 Should pre-school groups be family-centred using parental resources and developing the educational potential of parents to sustain the work of the groups?

2 Should pre-school groups be community-centred using the group as a

springboard for developing self-help within the community?

3 Should pre-school groups be school-centred, projecting the organizational requirements of the school and emphasizing the socializing influences of the group?

4 Should pre-school groups be part of an earlier weaning away of children from their parents, so providing more opportunities for the emancipation of parents?

5 Should pre-school groups be concerned with developing intellectual skills in children?

6 Should pre-school groups provide a caring atmosphere to compensate for stressful home conditions of some children?

7 Should pre-school groups be child-centred, using play to allow the child to develop in a natural spontaneous way?

8 Should pre-school groups be concerned with helping children's immediate development rather than hoping for long-term effects?

It will be seen that the items on this list are not mutually exclusive. They may be combined in different ways to suit the particular philosophy or needs of a local organization. The issues raised will be discussed in more detail in later chapters, together with a consideration of valid aims for different strategies.

Much of current plans and developments in provision for the under-fives is based on the expectation that earlier intervention will have a long-lasting influence on the child and will provide greater equality of opportunity for him. There is little evidence that earlier intervention has long-lasting effects on the performance or social adaptability of children.[10] Much more research into the development of young children is required, particularly in areas concerned with perception, motivation, and so on. Whether pre-school groups should be formed to meet the immediate needs of young children, rather than to lay down a foundation for their future development, will clearly affect the way strategies are determined.

The family-centred approach in fact sets a model which combines both short- and long-term objectives. Many families live in situations of oscillating stress points with rare moments of social harmony, particularly in areas where housing conditions are inadequate. For children who live in such a state of fluctuation there may be moments when a peaceful, cohesive environment is extremely valuable. Equally, there will be moments when children need to release tensions, which have built up before a group session. There is some evidence to suggest that children make slower responses during times of family stress.[11] The association between social stress and changes in response by parents and children has been an important and salutary lesson for teachers who, so far, have been involved in family-centred, pre-school activities. We suggest that any consideration of provision for children below school age should include a study of family interaction and development.

It is usual for teachers and nursery assistants to study child development during their training. Often a particular period in a child's development is studied and recorded during a college course. While this provides the student with good experience in observation and record-keeping concerning one child, the interaction of the child and the rest of the family is much more difficult to establish and is often missed. Yet the results of family interaction are crucial in understanding the behaviour patterns of a child.

Identity in the family

The teacher who is privileged and able to enter the family circle of a young child, either in a group or in a home, arrives at an important stage in the child's development. It is also important for the parents and grandparents. The child is building up an organized view of himself and the world surrounding him. He explores sensations, relationships and develops a personal identity. The mother is absorbed in her child's world, sharing his experiences and projecting her responses to his actions. Her view of the world changes as she adjusts to the new relationship with her child, and this affects the relationship she has with her husband. If the grandparents are alive and present their identity, too, will change as they form a relationship with the child. As Erik Erikson explains[12] their identity comes in part from a rearward look at their grandchild and his relationship with their own child.

Marjorie Boxall in her paper 'Multiple Deprivation: An Experiment in Nurture',[13] sums up the process.

> This sense of identity depends not only on the differentiation of a body image, distinction of inner world and outer world, self and other, but suffusing this the cohesive sustaining power of affectional bonds with the parents, with internalization of their attitudes and expectations, from which empathy, guilt and self control derive. It is through these early experiences and relationships that the child develops a body of valid and reinforcing schemata which will shape and determine later thought, feeling, attitudes and behaviour, and enable him when he goes to school, to use the situation he finds.

Where housing and social conditions are not conducive or where the parents are isolated or separated, many of the families do not develop the sense of identity described. Grandparents are not present to support parents. The child suffers from a limited experience as the pressures of living suppress the normal interaction between parents.

It is into situations such as this that the family-centred teacher[14] may enter. There may be nothing that she can do other than to make regular contact with the family. But in the majority of cases the teacher can halt the crippling effects which loss of identity can bring. By playing with the child in the home and by introducing toys and materials she helps the mother to revive an interest in her child's development. Working with mothers in the pre-school group she can provide a support system for those who need most help, by encouraging other mothers to take on the task.

The effect on her child of raising the morale of the mother can be great. It represents a therapeutic step which has a positive result with the rest of the family. It may be a first step towards a community consciousness and a realization of self-helping processes.

Within the family-centred approach to pre-school activities two bodies of theory merge. On the one hand we see the psychological influences working in the development of personality and learning procedures, on the other hand we can identify sociological factors which condition the family's outlook and produce internalized concepts of society. The following chapters consider each in turn together with the implications for parents and teachers.

The three case studies introduced at the beginning of this chapter describe the pre-school activities of John, Elaine and Robert, but the impact of, and on, the family was left implicit.

In John's case, no organizational structure was present which would allow him to develop in a sheltered environment apart from his home, for even a small part of his life, up to the age of five, when he would commence full-time schooling. Without adequate preparation he will enter a school situation which, to children better prepared by their families, will seem ordered and predictable. For John the school is a bewildering, exciting place which imposes control beyond his conceptual experience. He cannot identify boundaries set by the controls and so begins the painful business, for all concerned, of exploding violently in order to determine his reference points in acceptable behaviour, or he may withdraw completely.

Elaine's nursery class is representative of many well-equipped, caring, institutions which are being provided in most parts of the country in response to Department of Education and Science Circular 2/73, *Nursery Education*. Elaine is taken to the nursery class each day by her mother and left with the teacher. Although she has had a few tearful afternoons, Elaine has now settled well into the daily activities and she waits patiently to be collected by her mother or a neighbour at the end of the sessions. Not every child settles so well to the new situation away from her mother. With a younger age range of children being placed in situations which are away from the familiar context of home, siblings and parents, there is a greater probability that separation anxiety will be found, not only in the children but also in the parents.

Eisenberg's study[15] in the communication of anxiety contains a note of caution for all forms of intervention which affect family structure. Although his study considers school phobia and the psychiatric treatment of children referred from different parts of the school system, his thesis is concerned with the anxieties which are transferred by parents, mothers and fathers, to their children.

> Without exception, the mothers were anxious or ambivalent. Each gave a history of a poor relationship with her own mother: most were currently in the throes of a struggle to escape the over

protective domination of a mother or a mother-in-law.

Elaine is developing, within the nursery class, concepts of controls and behaviour which she has commenced to learn through interaction with her parents. She is becoming familiar with the boundaries which she will find later in school.

Robert, too, has had to make adjustments to his view of the world. His nursery group includes a number of adults, some of whom clearly 'belong' to individual children. His own mother plays with other children in the group rather than himself. He also has to share toys and to wait his turn for some activities. Sometimes he must sit quietly and listen to other children or his teacher. He is learning to be independent, to dress himself and use the lavatory without assistance from adults.

Both Robert and Elaine are undergoing a process of socialization which will enable them to accept full-time school more easily than John. They also have begun to develop skills of understanding and communication which are compatible with the requirements of school. They will both be in a better position to progress beyond the watershed mentioned earlier, at the age of five. It is likely, in Elaine's case, that the watershed has been moved to the point when she is three years old.

What are the objectives of such pre-school groups, in fact? It seems very possible, because of the background and training of the teachers involved, that nursery classes will be an extension of the school system which, for children like John, may allow him to conform to school requirements more easily. Such a result may be very commendable and would be applauded by many educationists; however it seems to us that instead of thinking in terms of a 'watershed' or 'bridging the gap between home and school' the powerful educative features of home and the influential educative features of school require to be fused together in such a way that the two overlap for a considerable period in a child's life. Such a policy may not be easily carried out since it implies considerable changes in attitude on the part of parents as well as by teachers. The chapters following discuss the implications of such changes and draw on the examples of strategies which are attempting a fusion process. It is already apparent that this process must continue well into the infant or first school.[16] We are suggesting therefore that the pre-school revolution could, if developed in imaginative ways, avoid being drowned in the back-wash of the school system, and produce its own 'bow-wave' effect, which may itself change that system into one which is responsive to both individual and community needs.

4

A structured approach to early education

During the past two decades an increasing number of research studies into various aspects of the development of young children have provided evidence for people interested in the promotion of early education programmes. Many such studies have actually set up programmes for young children, notably the research sponsored by the United States Office of Economic Opportunity which initiated the Head Start Program in 1965. The effect of this activity has been manifested in a cycle of propaganda, persuasion and interpretation of research findings which has been directed towards Government departments and particularly the Secretary of State for Education. The cycle has increased its speed of revolution in recent years but in the stillness of its centre many of those concerned with nursery education appear to be largely unmoved.

This chapter sets out to examine the evidence of research into the development of young children and includes comment on recent strategies used in early education programmes. It acknowledges the dedicated work of many teachers in nursery classes throughout the country and applauds the dynamic activism of the Pre-school Playgroups Association (PPA), which, together with other voluntary bodies, is providing a necessary service for many children at the present time. The review of current practice in nursery classes and playgroups contained in the next section, is not intended as a criticism of their operation but as a frame of reference within which the place of structured programmes may be examined.

The present situation in nursery and pre-school groups

The revived interest in early education during the past fifteen years has occurred for similar reasons to those which stimulated Froebel, Montessori and the McMillan sisters to advocate provision for young children. Social conditions in the nineteenth century had produced slum cultures which in turn led to serious human problems. Educational reform concerning the early childhood years was seen as a vital necessity in order to correct a lack of experience in cognitive manipulation which appeared to lead to incompetence and an undermining of self-esteem. Children from more affluent homes seemed better equipped to learn and understand.

The emphasis which Froebel placed on play has been maintained for many years in nursery schools in this country. The 'highly serious and deep significance of play' has been recognized as essential in nursery programmes and 'free play' is usually central to the curriculum. Breaks during a half-day session enable the children to group for teacher-led story, music or conversation periods, but teachers and assistants are aware of the need for children to develop language through their activities and aim therefore to create a climate which encourages easy communication at all times. Apparatus such as climbing frames, slides, play-houses, trolleys, trucks, swings and rocker-boats are commonly provided to encourage play which develops body-awareness, balance, judgment and to help children to establish good social relationships with others. Fine motor-skills are developed by using interlocking building kits, threading beads, painting, modelling, jigsaws, picture trays and insets. Such activities are linked with children's abilities to create, so, through play, opportunities are provided which develop imagination. Role play now forms an important part of nursery school activities and a 'dressing-up' box is a normal part of class equipment. 'Home corners' too are a very usual feature of nursery classrooms. Water and sand often are relegated to outside areas but nevertheless are seen as important materials for play by most teachers to help children develop concepts eventually of use to them in 'science'. Rooms are colourful and bright. Equipment and toys are normally presented in primary colours to help colour sense and matching. Pictures painted by children usually decorate walls and sometimes windows. In such environments teachers endeavour to provide enjoyable situations in which the children play and grow.

As children grow, so the nursery class is used to develop their social skills. Personal cleanliness is encouraged, shoes and coats are taken off and put on, food and milk are consumed in an orderly, mannerly way, toilets are used properly and efficiently. Considerable emphasis is placed on good social relationships within the group and a sense of individual independence is encouraged. The attitudes and feelings of young children during their first introduction to the school system are important and every effort is made, architecturally and by teachers, to invite them to participate in the joy of discovery, of observing, of experimenting and creating. School is an exciting place where children meet, discover and learn in comfortable, safe surroundings.

The role of the teacher in this situation is complex. The idea, generated by notions of 'free play and discovery', that the teacher is the passive observer of children's frolics, clearly must be discounted. Since she has created the environment which encourages the children's activities, she has given careful thought to the component parts of that environment and therefore is in control of it. She can introduce fresh components and remove over-familiar or unacceptable ones. But it is at the inter-personal level that her role assumes its most delicate attribute. She will need to understand the behaviour patterns of each of the children in her class and may frequently channel the attention of individuals who are not following acceptable social patterns of behaviour towards more positive, socially-conforming modes. This process can be physically and emotionally demanding. Nursery classes of three-and-a-half to four-and-a-half year old children do not, in the English nursery tradition, spend long periods of time concentrating on one activity but move quickly and often unpredictably between centres of interest. 'Accidents' with water, paint, clay or sand are not uncommon. It is within an atmosphere of bustle and noise that the teacher has to help children to manage their feelings, to make choices and decisions, to establish routines, to expect failure as well as success. At the same time she is helping children to develop intellectually at their own individual rates through exploration, investigation, assimilation and reflection. She must therefore decide on the degree to which she exercises leadership and control without removing initiative and freedom to experiment from the children.

In short, nursery schools and classes represent the first stage of a school system and, as such, are concerned with the socialization of children to prepare them for the next school stage. This process weans children away from home and dependence upon parents, often, in some areas, under conditions which are described as 'materially better than the children's homes'. In such areas of high social need, the Urban Aid programme has enabled local authorities to provide an increasing number of nursery classes following recommendations contained in the Plowden Report.[1] A very small percentage of under-five-year-olds have an opportunity to attend a free state-provided nursery class,[2] however, and this gross lack of provision stimulated voluntary bodies like the Save the Children Fund, the National Society for the Prevention of Cruelty to Children, the National Elfrida Rathbone Society and during the past twelve years, the PPA, to set up groups catering for the needs of pre-school-aged children.

The PPA is important, not only because of its origins as a grassroots movement, but also because it sets out to meet the needs of mothers and children together. Since Belle Tutaev's letter to the *Guardian* in 1961, describing her playgroup, the movement has expanded to a national organization catering for a large proportion of the 250,000 children who attend registered groups.[3] Advice is given to adults, usually mothers, who wish to set up playgroups in their area, courses of instruction for group leaders, assistants and parents are organized on a regional and county basis. Area organizers and local advisers, many supported by local authority grants, help to maintain standards of operation within groups, liaising with local authority departments and schools. One of the chief concerns of the movement, however, is to support and encourage mothers in their parental role. Playgroups therefore contribute to a more varied provision for under-fives than would have existed a few years ago. They help to meet particular needs—for groups of handicapped children, children in hospital, foster children, and for particular areas—rural communities, high-rise flats, housing estates and dormitory suburbs.

In spite of a very diverse range of circumstances under which the groups operate, there is, implicit in the very name of the movement, an emphasis on play and creativity. It is interesting to note that 'Froebel-trained' teachers were members of the 1973 executive committee and a considerable proportion of the area organizers have had nursery-teaching experience. A well-run pre-school group will be little different in its activities and equipment from a state-supported nursery class. Certainly its objectives in providing opportunities for children's 'deep personal discovery and experiment' are the same. Its difference may lie in the degree to which parents are involved in its operation and certainly lies in the reliance placed upon their financial support through fees or fund-raising ventures.

Management of activities and children within groups remains a problem for many group leaders who find the delicate balance between freedom of expression and anarchy difficult to maintain. In her book *The Playgroup Movement*, Brenda Crowe[4] gives a frank account of her experiences in visiting groups where such difficulties exist and she draws attention to the task of the movement in training both leaders and parents to understand processes of learning and teaching. Later in the book she describes the disenchantment of members taking part in training courses, with psychologists who fail to give clear, decisive instructions on methods of dealing with 'difficult children', but instead concentrate on child development studies.

This attitude towards psychological studies is significant, especially since recent research into cognitive and conceptual abilities of young children provides much thought-provoking evidence. The next section discusses some studies, but it is necessary, before moving to the discussion, to complete the frame of reference within which it takes place.

A proportion of two-to-five-year-olds attend day-care nurseries or live in residential homes for young children. The majority of day-care nurseries are the direct responsibility of Social Service Departments. Their main function is to care for children of single-parent families during working hours or to care for children in great social need. Places are provided on a scale of charges according to family means. A matron is usually in charge of the nursery and she is assisted by experienced, and student, nursery nurses, who are responsible for programmes of activities with the children. The provision includes meals and rest rooms for the children. Recently, local authorities with day-care responsibility have become more interested in the content of daily programmes of activity carried out in nurseries, following the results of the Hillfields Centre Project in Coventry which combines day-care with normal nursery school facilities. It is becoming clear that catering for the physical and emotional needs of young children can be combined with provision for their intellectual needs.

The care of children during periods when parents may be working is one of the functions of pre-school provision. Demand far exceeds supply, however, and the childminding process has grown rapidly in recent years. Brian Jackson's[5] estimate of 100,000 children placed in the daily care of unofficial childminders, is a good example of the imbalance of provision for the under-fives. This figure is five times the present number of places available in day-care nurseries and contains a large proportion of children living in urban centres and belonging to West Indian or West African families. It is unlikely that these children will receive adequate intellectual, physical or emotional stimuli comparable with those received by children living in more affluent areas.

The arguments which support programmes of pre-school provision in areas of social need have been well rehearsed and generally accepted. Consideration of inequality of opportunity leads to thoughts on factors affecting the processes of child development and it is to this subject that the discussion now turns.

Cognitive development and concept formation in young children

> The tide and trend of pre-school development may be outlined tersely, as follows:
> In the first quarter of the first year the infant gains control of twelve tiny muscles which move his eyes.
> In the second quarter (16-28 weeks) he comes into command of the muscles which support his head and move his arms. He reaches out for things.
> In the third quarter (28-40 weeks) he gains command of his trunk and hands. He sits. He grasps, transfers and manipulates objects. In the fourth quarter (40-52 weeks) he extends command to his legs and feet; to his forefinger and thumb. He pokes and plucks. He stands upright.
> In the second year he walks and runs; articulates words and phrases; acquires bowel and bladder control; attains a rudimentary sense of personal identity and of personal possession. In the third year he speaks in sentences, using words as tools of thought; he shows a positive propensity to understand his environment and to comply with cultural demands. He is no longer a 'mere' infant.
> In the fourth year he asks innumerable questions, perceives analogies, displays an active tendency to conceptualise and generalise. He is nearly self-dependent in the routines of home life.
> At five he is well matured in motor control. He hops and skips. He talks without infantile articulation. He can narrate a long tale. He prefers associative play; he feels socialized pride in clothes and accomplishment. He is a self-assured, conforming citizen in his small world.

Arnold Gesell's[6] dramatic summary of the growth pattern, which he derived from his clinical studies of young children, is useful in placing a discussion of cognitive development into perspective. The overriding concept produced by studies of the age group 0-5 is of growth, not only from the rapid increases in size and weight, particularly during the first two years of life, but also in the organizing processes of growth. As the child's sensory and motor skills develop so his awareness of himself and his relationship with other people alters. Profound changes take place within this period of development which are never equalled later in life. But most dramatic of all in any consideration of the formative years must be the divergence of human development even from birth. A point to be borne in mind with Gesell's summary is that it need not be taken as a norm with which to compare children's development from widely differing backgrounds. Not only is physical development a considerable variant between children in this age group but so too is mental growth, use of language and adaptive behaviour. Furthermore the development rates of each of these factors are not constant within individuals. The reasons for such spurts may be due to genetic or environmental reasons or both, but the fact remains that unevenness of growth exists within young children. A smooth linear development of perceptual and cognitive skill does not occur naturally or at a predictable rate. In a sense, therefore, the view presented by Gesell provides a useful caveat when theories of cognitive development are being considered.

An infant of six months has learned from his experience of a feeding bottle and has already commenced the development of sensory, motor, perceptual skills in touching, gripping, sucking and identifying the bottle. The bottle also produces an emotional response, especially when it becomes empty. The rate at which the development of these skills takes place is fast and must be simultaneous as the infant receives and uses the bottle. His competence in using the bottle is the result of his own organizing process which links responses, enables him to feed and feel satisfied.

Precisely how an infant begins to build a theory of his environment is at present unknown. Laboratory work conducted by Munday-Castle and Anglin[7] is typical of recent experiments to identify anticipation of events by infants from ten days to five months old. Two windows are presented to the child alternately containing vivid visual objects which appear in regular succession. He soon learns to look where the object appears after scanning both windows and develops the skill of monitoring the blank window with a quick eye movement.

Experiments at the University of Edinburgh using infants of a similar age show that they are capable of learning to manipulate buzzers and electric lights by head movements. Initially the child learns that by moving his head to the left, a light comes on over his cot. When he moves his head to the right, it goes out. Later sequences expect two head movements in one direction to operate the light.

The evidence from both series of experiments suggests that children are absorbed by their task and learn to anticipate the results of their operations. J.S. Bruner[8] describes signs of pleasure when infants learn to bring a motion picture into focus by sucking above a certain rate of a blind nipple. The infants smile when they have mastered the technique, possibly displaying early signs of the self-rewarding property of learning found later in life.

However rudimentary such experiments may seem, they represent important steps in providing a picture of the thought processes of very young infants before speech develops. This information is useful when considering theories of cognitive development. Piaget[9] divides intellectual development into four periods; a sensori-motor period, a pre-operational period, a period of concrete operations and a period of formal operations. Each of these periods is derived from the way in which the child organizes his knowledge of himself and the world around him. The way in which thought is organized is central to this theory.

During the sensori-motor period, said by Piaget to cover the first two years of life, cycles of activity are discovered and repeated by the infant. The repetition of actions which have developed into voluntary movements from early reflexes give evidence of the existence of a primitive memory. Between four and eight months attention is directed to objects outside his body and the infant's actions become more generalized to include anything within reach. Later still intervening objects are moved in order to reach desired objects which suggests that his thought and action are being co-ordinated in a systematic or schematic way. Between twelve and eighteen months the child can devise ways of attaining goals by modifying and experimenting with existing schemata. During this period the child's speech begins to develop and he commences to represent objects in symbolic and mental images. He can now accommodate himself to new situations as he modifies known situations. By the age of two years the child can imitate and copy the actions of persons and through his modified behaviour copy their actions, even though they are not present.

There may well be times within the sensori-motor stage when it would be opportune to present a child with processes to develop certain functions. It is interesting to note that in the Soviet handbook[10] for pre-school education, 'instructresses' are advised, when working with babies aged ten months to one year, to follow activities and games to develop speech such as 'show me your ears', naming toys, playing with animals, 'find and bring me the toy'. In activities to develop manipulation, fitting and stacking toys are demonstrated to and used by the children. Performing such operations involves identifying and selecting objects according to their shape and size. Such tasks also require persistence on the part of the baby especially when selection of objects to complete an action is required, as in finding a lid for a box or saucepan.

In Piaget's outline of the young child's development he suggests that following, but not entirely displacing, the sensori-motor stage, a child enters a preparatory period from two years through to four years when his thought processes gradually move towards higher levels of representation. Before turning to a consideration of the pre-operational stage in a child's development, it is important to emphasize that the first two years of life are crucial in determining later physical, emotional and intellectual patterns. The socialization and learning processes begin as soon as a child is born. They begin in the home. If the home is not conducive to the forms of early learning mentioned then some ground will have been lost before the child is three. The key role played by parents in this development will be discussed later in this chapter and, of course, the intervention and stimulus provided by parents continues to be vital through the pre-operational, concrete operations and formal operations stages of a child's development.

Most children attending pre-school groups will have reached a stage in which their intellectual growth results in their ability to create meaningful personal representations of themselves and their environment and to relate such representations to each other. Such relationships are a critical aspect of cognitive development. The ability to recognize the various sensations received by sense organs and then to organize them into a framework accurately and consistently is of vital importance to learning. In addition to the organization of sensations received, an adaptation process occurs so that incoming knowledge is adapted to the child's view of the world and his view of the world is adapted to the new knowledge. This implies that cognition is guided by perception. Children think intuitively, at this stage. They have a tendency to focus attention on specific static objects within the environment. They see at the moment what is real for them and do not consider changes which may occur. Indeed it is usual for a child's attention to focus first on one object and then on a second object without establishing any logical connection between the two. Each point of focus is seen as a separate entity, which is compartmentalized into a series of pictures, providing a constant revision but no recording of this revision.

Until reversibility of thought takes place, enabling a child to record changes in the environment by referring back to previous focus points which have been internalized as mental images, then the child has a fleeting grasp of concepts. It is here that the use of language helps a child to compare things, which demands reasoning. A child who cannot use language may be discriminating between things at a perceptual level only. During the period from two to three years of age a major development in the use of words takes place as the child is able to convey increasing information about his intention and point of view. Initially his attempts to communicate will include many gestures and actions, but as he decodes the components of speech received from others around him, he begins to use adjectives and pronouns, particularly 'it' and 'that'. By three years six months, many children have established a number of the characteristics of adult speech and they will have established sets of meanings from their own experiences which will form the basis of their language.

> It is in word meanings that thought and speech unite into verbal thoughts. A word in this sense does not refer to a single object but to a group or class of objects. Each word is therefore already a

> generalisation. Thus generalisation can be said to be a verbal act of thought and reflects reality in quite another way than sensation and perception reflect it.[11]

Vygotsky's statement is closely linked with the stages in intellectual development so far discussed, for the language used by a child provides unmistakable clues to his ability to think. The curves of development in speech and thought remain apart, until eighteen months to two years, then join to form a new, enhanced perspective as the child discovers that each thing has a name. Throughout the pre-operational stage the child moves from an affective-connotative level to an intellectual level where his thought becomes verbal and his speech rational. It will be clear however that such an intellectual level will rarely be reached by a child of pre-school age. Indeed, Piaget divides the pre-operational stage into two parts:

'pre-conceptual'—mental age range two–four years;
'intuitive'—mental age range four–seven years.

The concern of this chapter is the development of children aged up to five years and it follows that most attention will be paid in this discussion to children who have reached the pre-conceptual level since it is this group who may be receiving forms of early education.

As the name 'pre-conceptual' implies, children at this stage are not yet able to formulate concepts in the same manner as older children and adults. Concepts or abstract thinking can be described as 'skills involving the ability to organize thoughts, to reflect on situations, to comprehend the meaning of events and to structure behaviour so as to be able to choose alternatives'. 'Pre-concepts' are formed by 'transductive' reasoning in which children move from one instance to another particular instance. For example Anne, a three-year-old, went on holiday at Easter time and received an Easter egg. She then persistently asked her father for another holiday in order to receive another egg. Holiday and egg occur together once, therefore they occur together for all time.

During this stage the child is unable to see things from the other person's viewpoint, since he cannot understand that the other's view will be different from his own. 'Egocentricism' is therefore a common feature, usually manifested in rehearsing speech with himself. Lisa, a three-year-old, was overheard to say to herself, during a pre-school group session, 'of course, everyone loves me', in a serious and totally believing way.

Piaget draws a distinction between performance at a motoric level and verbal performance. Until a child has language, his manipulation of his environment is entirely physical. As was mentioned earlier, language is important in extending mental representations, although a child must have reached a certain capacity to make mental pictures before language can be developed.

Gesell's study[12] indicates that at the age of two years many children have commenced a period of transition, particularly as far as language is concerned. A wide variability in size of vocabulary was found with a group of twenty-eight cases producing a range from 5 to 1,212 words. He also recorded an increase in the use of word combinations over younger groups of children, although their use of compound sentences was rare, some children were using sentences containing simple phrases. However, towards three years a marked progress is noticed towards an integration with the total behaviour of the child.

> Vocabulary is extensive; long sentences including compound and complex structures are common; tense, moods, and parts of speech are distinguished, however imperfectly. Generalisation is common, and both in talking and in comprehension of the speech of others, non-present situations are dealt with verbally (p. 13).

A wide difference in language responses was noted including many whose language was still representative of children six months younger.

At four years many children have commenced to use words in a flowing way, questioning persistently, verbalizing situations frequently. Gesell records that it is common for drawings to be named in advance although they undergo changes of name as the drawing proceeds. Drawings often provide the starting point of elaborated descriptions or anecdotes and this process gives important clues to the ability of children to verbalize their mental representations.

In summary, if Piaget's theory of cognitive development is followed, a child entering a pre-school group at the age of two years has reached the threshold of the second stage in a sequence of mental growth. The experiences of the first, sensori-motor stage have prepared and provided a base for the second stage. During this stage the child will develop capabilities which enable him to link actions to actions, things to things, things to actions. He will organize his relationships with things and develop mental representations of himself and his environment in an increasingly abstract way, by action, by image and by symbol.

But what happens to the child who has not reached the level of 'readiness' described by Piaget even though his chronological age may enable him to attend pre-school? Gesell's clinical studies show wide differences, in all the areas examined, in a number of his cases. A number of programmes have been carried out in recent years to attempt to accelerate the intellectual development of children who for environmental or genetic reasons are classed 'disadvantaged'. Further studies have compared children from working-class and middle-class backgrounds, defined in terms of fathers' occupations, and have shown marked differences in performance, even at an early age. Large factors such as social class, however, often obscure the fact that wide differences occur within social classes and particularly within family environments. It may follow therefore that the lessons learned during the programmes for specific groups of children may have wider relevance for numbers of under-fives who will attend nursery or playgroups in the future.

Developments in early education programmes

Marion Blank's[13] work on methods of fostering abstract thinking in young children provides an excellent corollary to a discussion concerning conceptual development. Her programme with a group of disadvantaged children commenced in 1967 in order to examine a methodology which would help children to develop internal symbolic sytems. Accordingly an individual teaching programme was designed in order to counter an important effect of group programmes, i.e. that individuals whose cognitive functioning is underdeveloped, can pass unnoticed in the normal nursery situation, since symbolic functioning need have no outward display.

Daily teaching sessions of fifteen to twenty minutes were held with individual children who then returned to the group situation. Much depended upon the technique of the teacher during these sessions and the two transcripts which follow later are intended to provide a clearer picture of the questioning and listening required in order for effective dialogue to be produced between teacher and child.

The programme focused on a small area of human behaviour in a detailed analytical way. Intellectual skills were considered under three main headings:

1 cognitively-directed perception;
2 the coding process;
3 problem-solving abilities.

A number of techniques were devised to help children overcome difficulties they experienced in making their perceptions meaningful:

1a Selective attention–the child was asked to make choices after comparing objects in order to foster the recognition of significant perceptual features.

1b Reduction of visual dominance–tasks were devised to enable the child to focus on sound and touch properties of objects.

1c Reduction of egocentric perspective–the magnetism of perceptual stimuli for young children seems related to the phenomenon of egocentricism. Role play helped to achieve a 'psychological distance' between stimuli and child.

1d Recognition of significant characteristics of objects and events–intellectual questioning. Child will be led to question unusual, new objects.

1e Recognition of the tangential from the germane–the child sees all elements of a situation having equal significance. Focus is placed on a main theme in questions.

1f Rationale for observations and behaviour–child often fails to isolate components perceived.

1g Awareness of learning–the child is not simply the passive recipient of instructions but takes an active role in learning.

2a Development of verbal concepts–following Bereiter and Engelmann,[14] the type of concept taught could be labelled simply. For example, in the case of polar definitions, up would be taught in contrast to not up rather than to down. Multiple concepts, linkage concepts, and definition through function were also taught.

2b Categories of exclusion–once a concept is well established it no longer requires great mental effort. Concepts were structured to achieve abstractions; e.g. draw something other than a circle.

2c Relation of the word to its referent–both in its fusion to a referent and in its separation–a word may be linked by a common denominator, e.g. tooth-paste, tooth-brush. The child's process of ordering may be helped in a logical way.

2d Relevant inner verbalization–child is trained to resort to inner verbalization by a number of exercises expecting internal manipulation of words.

2e Development of coding process–nonverbalized methods of coding information, e.g. drawing maps.

2f Awareness of possessing language–child may lack awareness that he possesses the skill of making an appropriate response.

3a Development of memory–in order to solve problems child requires to draw upon stored information.

3b Models for cause and effect reasoning–child requires to have the concrete illustration present and attention is focused on the new skill alone.

3c Imagery of future events–critical to cause and effect is the ability to image the outcome, e.g. where would the box be if it fell from the table?

3d Validation of verbal statements–clichéed response is inadequate for problem-solving requirements.

3e Recognition of the incorrect–child who cannot abstract finds the notion of right or wrong solutions in any given situation, difficult to understand.

3f Flexibility in thinking–child may think that there is only one appropriate response in any situation.

3g Selection of alternatives–child may not be able to think of a response and is given alternatives from which to choose.

3h Development of sequential ordering–a limitation of the thinking of young children lies in their difficulty in analysing the parts of a whole.

3i Development of a problem-solving strategy–child requires the ability to reflect on alternative courses of action.

3j Deductive and inductive reasoning–child requires skills of memory, categorization, elimination of irrelevant or incorrect information for this process.

3k Ability to employ sustained sequential thinking–to be able to see objects, events and issues as located within their appropriate framework the child requires concentration and the ability to shift flexibly from one skill to another.

3l Ability to sustain independent work–abstract thinking does not exist if external support must be supplied constantly.

The pilot programme developing the above intellectual skills involved a group of twelve three-to-four-year-old children. The following extracts[15] from two sessions usefully describe the procedure recommended by the programme and also provide an illustration of the need for highly-trained teachers to carry out this work.

The following dialogue with Julie is from a session held three months after the commencement of the programme. After entering the room, the teacher says:

Teacher Do you remember what we did when you were here yesterday?	The type of recall expected by now from the child extends over greater time spans but is still verifiable. By contrast, in the early session, recall was restricted to tasks in the immediate session.
Julie Yes.	
Teacher What did we do?	
Julie I don't know.	Despite her affirmative answer, the automatic negative response follows.
Teacher Let's see if I can help you. Is there anything on this table that we worked with the last time? (A limited variety of materials is present.)	Teacher presents visual aid to prod memory.
Julie (Points to blackboard.)	Child's gesture is correct.
Teacher That's just pointing. Tell me what we did.	Although a gesture would have been acceptable in an earlier session, teacher now demands a description since the child is capable of responding in language.
Julie We did–we did a square.	Without being given any hints, the child describes the correct object that she drew.
Teacher Right. What did we do with the square?	The teacher is making the child recount the next step in the past sequence.
Julie (Hesitates.)	
Teacher Think about it for a minute.	Teacher makes a judgment that the child can answer and delays offering help.
Julie We took it off. (Child refers to erasing.)	The pause has offered the child a chance to reflect. Her impulsive first answer has been replaced by accurate memory.
Teacher Good. Now, what did we use to take it off?	Teacher is continuing to focus on inter-related sequence of past events.
Julie I don't know.	
Teacher (Brings blackboard forward.) All right–what would you do if you had a	Since the child is encountering difficulty, the teacher chooses a slightly easier level by offering a

square on here and you wanted to get rid of it? How could you get it off?	question which has several alternative answers (i.e. 'What could you use to get it off?'). The child is thereby no longer limited to the past where only one answer (the thing that actually happened) is correct.
Julie Maybe we could use paper.	Child is more successful with this relaxation in demand.
Teacher Why could we use paper? What would it do?	Teacher's question is to make child aware of the relationship between the object and the action for which it can be used.
Julie It could take it off. It could rub it off.	Child grasps this connection and expresses herself in clear language.

The following extract records a session conducted by a visiting nursery teacher. It illustrates why a 'one-to-one' situation (so often advocated by educationists as the ultimate teaching situation for 'slow' children), fails to develop thinking skills. It is also a good example of the child-centred philosophy found in many nursery schools; 'what does the child want to do?' is the pervasive element.

An interchange about flowers ensued on the assumption that the child, in fact, had something definite she wanted to draw. The teacher did attempt to stimulate the child's recall of the specific flower but for this purpose again used unverifiable questions. After the child had drawn several flowers the teacher said:

Teacher Do you know how many flowers you have there now?	Teacher here is attempting to lead the child away from narrowness of flowers *per se* and integrate it with another concept i.e., number.
Julie Three. I'm five years old.	Child's association of one number with another has an understandable basis. However, her spontaneous use of the same words for a variety of phenomena (age, objects, etc.) suggests that she does not have a clear understanding of the concept of number. Although one would not expect greater understanding in a young child, one must be aware that confusion exists.
Teacher You're five years old? Maybe you could make flowers for how old you are. Do you	The teacher assumes that the child can make an equation between numbers in terms of

know how many more you would need?	years and numbers of objects.
Julie Five.	Child does not answer question, but rather repeats her response.
Teacher Five altogether. And how many do you have here?	Teacher makes attempt to dissect the problem for simplification. However, the complexity involved requires an almost endless dissection, e.g. 'five equals the number of years you are; each flower represents one year; the flowers do not equal the desired number of years; additional flowers must be drawn; you need to consider the number of flowers you have drawn relative to the desired number five, etc.' This fantastic complexity is far beyond the child's ability but is in effect what has been asked of her.
Julie I'll make one more. What kind of brown is this? It's a tree.	Child shows a primitive understanding that more is needed but not specifically how much or why. Her leading back to colour may be a combination of avoiding a difficult issue and another intrusion of an impulsive idea.
Teacher Oh that's pretty, Julie. That's very, very nice.	Topic of numbers had been discarded without any advance in child's knowledge.
Julie I bet it's time to wake up now.	Child is referring to the nap time of the rest of the nursery group.
Teacher What time do you get up?	Teacher has misinterpretated child's reference to mean time she wakes up at home. This confusion is reasonable and where teaching time is unlimited, it is of no special significance. In a language programme with a highly restricted time element, however, it hampers the few opportunities available to teach a child how to interpret correctly other people's frames of reference.
Julie I get up five o'clock.	It is likely that child is perseverating the 'five' from the earlier discussion.

Teacher In the morning (incredulously). Do you really wake up at five o'clock in the morning?
Julie I do.
Teacher And what time do you come to school?
Julie I don't know what time . . . night-time?
Teacher No.
Julie I think so; I got a clock. I'm tired.

This dialogue again illustrates the type of communication between a child and teacher which is often mistaken for a conceptual discussion (i.e. time, hours, daytime, night-time, etc.).
Child's lack of awareness of the absurdity of being in nursery school at night indicates that she is in a discussion beyond her depth. In her effort to respond, child is led to rely on prattle alone.

This brief description of Marion Blank's programme can achieve little more than to provide an outline of its philosophy and operation. Two factors emerge which are fundamental and practical in terms of replicating similar schemes elsewhere. How can a nursery teacher find time to work in a systematic individual way? Where are teachers to be found who are trained to work in this way?

At Red House Education Centre, Teresa Smith[16] set up an 'individual language programme' for pre-school-age children in 1970. Her work was based on Marion Blank's experience in New York but the programme included students in training, to act as teachers during its second phase, conducted on school premises. It was therefore possible to carry out an experimental programme to develop techniques and experience in individual work and to assess its value as a method of both diagnosing the children's skill level and improving those skills. It was possible to examine the relationship between group work and individual work and also the practical problems of such involvement. Finally the programme allowed the training of teachers for individual work and their operation within a normal day school to be observed.

The aims of the programme included:

developing the child's problem-solving abilities—to use abstract rather than concrete levels of thought;
sustaining the child's concentration;
sustaining independent work;
developing response to adults;
improving communication generally;
developing co-operation with other children.

It was necessary for the teacher to consider each session in a dual way: first, the process which the child would carry out, e.g. comparing differences between two things, and second, the skill which was being developed in the child.

The list of skills to be introduced and developed by the programme followed Blank quite closely but was grouped slightly differently. Tape recordings were made of each session and transcribed for the next session in order that the teacher could possess an accurate record upon which the next session could be structured. Each child received two sessions per week over a period of one school year (forty weeks).

Pre- and post-testing of the children was carried out as part of an overall research programme for pre-school children in the area.[17]

The following transcript is typical of a session and presents an interesting comparison with the American study:

Name Darren	*Date* Tuesday, 16 March 1971
Theme Pegs and pegboard	*Age* 5·2

D. I can do them mosaic things. I can make patterns.
T. Well I thought we would do something a little different today Darren. What are these?
D. Pegs and pegboards. Them's alright. They stick in little holes. You can make them into patterns. Animals and colours.
T. (using small pegboard) Where am I putting this red peg, Darren?
D. Up at top.
T. Can you put a red peg in the same place on your pegboard?
T. Is it exactly in the same place as mine, Darren?
D. Course, 'cos it's right next to yours and it's red and it's the same.
T. But my red peg is at the top left hand corner. Where's yours?
D. I don't know what to call it . . . corner. It's that one. It's not left.
T. Where will your red peg have to go to make it like mine?
D. Move it from the left.
T. Where have you moved it to, Darren?
D. Told you I don't know what to call it.
T. That's the right hand corner, Darren.
D. I know left hands.
T. Put a black peg on the left hand side, Darren and a black peg opposite it on the right side.
D. Done that, you do it.
T. Is that the same as yours Darren?
D. You've gone one up at your side.
T. Which side is that Darren?
D. Over on your side.
T. If I hide my pegboard and have some pegs, will you tell me where to put them so that my pegboard will look just like yours when we have finished?
D. Ready? It's red and it goes in the top hand corner (speaking distinctly, just as if he is now trying to mimic the way I had been speaking to him. I had tried to be very clear and precise—I felt sure Darren was trying hard to do the same).

T. In the top hand corner?
D. In the top left hand corner.
T. That's very clear, Darren. Good boy. What's your next one?
D. It goes in the other top corner. Right. Right (shouts excitedly).
T. Good boy, Darren. What colour is your peg?
D. It's right. It goes in that corner. Oh, it's black.
T. I've put the black peg in the top corner on the right side.
D. Now it's yellow in the bottom hand, right, right corner.
T. Good boy, Darren, I've done that one.
D. The bottom left side corner has got a blue one. There's a blue one in the middle. I'll put a yellow one down that side.
T. Which side?
D. Down the right corner side.
T. How many holes shall I miss?
D. Peg, space, space, there. (Darren continues with clear instructions.)
T. Shall we check the pegboards now and see if they are the same?
D. I bet they will be the same. Yes, they are, 'cos I said where to go. Can I hide away?
(Darren carefully stands a box in the middle of the table and puts an arm round his pegboard so that I can't see it at all. When we check after I have called out six peg positions he is right.)
D. Our Shaun will be over there in that room. I don't think he can see down here.
T. I should think Shaun will be very busy this morning. Do you think Shaun will know left side and right side and the corners?
D. I should think so. But I do 'cos I know them now when I play. I can't draw pegs to show Miss D.—oh well she isn't here. I can't draw left pegs and that.
T. Do you think we can tell Mrs E. all about the corners and the pegs?
D. 'Cos she might be busy though. It's busy today. (When we got back into the classroom, the children have various games, etc. out. Darren goes to the pegs and pegboard and puts pegs in the corners but doesn't now seem to want to talk about them, just quietly plays.)

The important difference between the two studies so far described is that the Denaby Main children have received follow-up testing each year since 1970 in school and it has therefore been possible to identify differences in performance across various groups who took part in other programmes in the area. The division into groups was made on a 'matched pairs' basis using pre-test scores on English Picture Vocabulary Test (EPVT), so that the average pre-test scores of the individually tutored group and the control group were therefore similar and establish a good basis for post-test comparison. At post-test the average difference between the groups was large (over 6 points) in favour of the tutored group, as the West Riding EPA Project Final Report establishes. The 1972[18] follow-up figures show that the lead on EPVT is maintained at about 5 points of standard score, the tutored group averaging about 100 once again.

The limitations of specially trained staff and time requirements have inhibited replication on a wider scale of individual tutoring. A number of structured schemes have been devised, however, to be used by teachers and leaders of playgroups. Dr Simon Haskell's and Margaret Paull's[19] schemes for training basic motor skills and basic cognitive skills are a good example.

The basic cognitive skills scheme is presented as a training programme of pre-reading exercises for children aged between two and six years, to develop competence in perceptual discrimination, concept formation, sequential reasoning, eye–hand co-ordination, etc. The exercises are produced in a series of twenty-eight booklets which are intended to be used by individual children but also help the teacher to devise a flexible programme around them, since the booklets are graded in categories such as 'position', 'sequence', 'size', 'perception', etc.

Haskell and Paull's scheme for motor skill development in young children follows a similar method to the cognitive skills scheme, of presenting booklets to be used by individuals who are required to follow a series of exercises which practise hand–eye co-ordination and control in the form of pre-writing skills.

Both schemes were introduced at Red House during 1972-3 and parents were trained to use them with their own children who attended the regular pre-school group. Parents and children then used the booklets at home throughout the year. It was found to be possible to conduct the normal group activities and use the scheme on an individual basis quite effectively, mainly because of the interest shown by the parents combined with the positive response of the children to the work.

An increasing number of programmes recognize the need to involve, or train parents, in pre-school activities at home. Caldwell,[20] Gordon,[21] Gray and Klaus,[22] Weikart and Lambie,[23] in the USA, Lombard[24] in Israel, Kellaghan[25] in Eire, Halsey[26] in this country, have reported on the results of work in this field. In general mothers of disadvantaged children have been found to be both interested in and capable of active involvement in the process of education especially when carried out informally. The strategies used in the programmes vary, some using trained teachers to work in the home of young children, others training 'community aides' led by professionals. The majority rely upon some form of individualized programmed instruction, which is administered during regular weekly sessions lasting about one hour with each child.

Lombard's report[27] on 'Home Instruction Program for Pre-school Youngsters' (HIPPY), describes an instructional programme which focused on three major areas of intellectual fuctioning: formal language, sensory discrimination and problem solving. Commercially prepared story books were used to develop formal language by examining the sequence, details, vocabulary and new concepts contained in the stories. Games and exercises were designed from the results of this examination to provide new experiences.

Visual, auditory and tactile discrimination were essential components of the programme, using exercises requiring 'same-different' discrimination in which the children were taught to identify critical attributes of materials presented. The ability to list the attributes of objects or ideas and the ability to pair or group objects or ideas, were encouraged as a necessary requirement for problem solving.

Lessons to be given by the community aides or the mothers were written in full detail by the research team.

> The format used indicated the instructor's actions and words, the expected response of the child, and the instructor's corrective feedback. Since the program was designed for subprofessionals, emphasis was placed on consistent feedback under all circumstances. Whereas a professional might be able to pick up a child's incorrect response and use it as a spring-board for teaching, we could not expect this from either the subprofessional aides or the mothers.[28]

A guide sheet for the mother covering the day's work and a weekly programme packet containing worksheets and materials were left in each home.

The programme was well accepted by the families taking part, who expressed willingness to continue for a further year. Post-test scores obtained in Frostig parts I and IV, Matrix, same-different, shapes and colours, showed the highest gains from the home instruction group against a school instruction group and a control group.

Nearer home an educational visiting scheme was commenced in Denaby Main during 1970[29] and continued as an experimental programme until July 1973. Based on Red House, a visitor worked with groups of families in the town. The families were selected using two criteria, age of the pre-school child visited and geographical location. Following a short pilot study, a main study was set up to include twenty children aged between 18 and 24 months living in one school catchment area. A control group was established in a town some miles away, consisting of socially matched families. The programme differed considerably in its method of presentation from the 'HIPPY' project, since the visitor decided, from her diagnosis of each family situation, on appropriate lessons to be carried out week by week, with the child and its parents. Much time was spent in showing the parents the importance of their role as educators of their children and they were encouraged to use books, materials and games in playing with their families.

Later in the programme a second main study was set up in a slightly more structured way. Kits of materials containing paint, blocks, beads, brushes, etc., were given to each family and a further resource bank of games, books and equipment was built up by the visitor. Items from the resource bank were listed with the development of specific cognitive skills detailed beside them, in order to assist easy reference. The visitor's time to be spent with each family was limited to one hour per week and in order to help her initial diagnosis of each child's ability, an 'indicator' was devised to provide a crude idea of motor and cognitive skill development.

The indicator is based on the 'draw-a-man' test and can be used with children aged 36-42 months. The child is first asked to draw a picture of a man, on paper provided. The child is then shown a picture of a man, supposedly drawn by the visitor and is asked to point to detailed parts of the man's dress. A verbal response is then expected in answer to questions such as 'what has the man got in his hand?' A symbolic picture of a man is shown to the child and he is asked to fit a series of coloured shapes over the picture. To be placed correctly the pieces require an increasing degree of fine motor skill. The child is asked to name the colours of the pieces, in turn, and finally is asked to judge whether the man's arm is longer than his leg, etc. The recorded responses provide the visitor with an impression of the child's manipulative skill, colour concept, positional concept, shape concept and his verbal skill. In other words, it is a tool for helping to provide an appropriate programme for the child and not an educational test.

The indicator was found to be a useful aid and has since been tried in similar schemes in other parts of the country.

The results of Merril Palmer tests taken during the Red House programme showed impressive performance gains over children in the control group, at the end of the first year. It is important, however, to treat test scores obtained with such young children cautiously, since several of the children were at the lower limit of the test's age range–being just eighteen months old.

In all the schemes so far described a monitoring of the progress of individuals has been carried out. The continuous monitoring was a requirement not only for evaluation of the programme on its completion, but also in order that the teacher could ensure that her input was matching the responses of individual children.

Implications for pre-school group leaders

A number of the intervention programmes listed or described in the preceding section have specific goals of achievement often in very limited areas of intellectual functioning. Once a goal is established, a structure of detailed stages is designed to help the child reach the goal. The rule always applied in the design of such a structure is 'move from the simple to the complex'. Weikart claims that although a teacher may plan and use her classroom within a definite structure she has the freedom to apply her skills creatively. She is the planner, operator and observer of an organic situation.

A common response from teachers of young children to notions of working within a theoretical framework is that providing a warm setting, well equipped for many activities and interaction with other children, allows the child to learn spontaneously and at his own rate. Yet within two years goals are being set. The usual and predominant one is the attainment of reading skill by the age of seven. This most complex skill combines perceptual, motor, verbal, positional skill at a representational level. The fashion of 'readiness' has caused difficulty for many teachers working with children, who, in Piagetian terms, are reaching the concrete operational level. The assumption is often made that children will have developed the necessary skills of perception and cognition spontaneously to enable them eventually to crack the reading code.

The work carried out with young children and their parents in the Red House pre-school group has demonstrated that it is possible to introduce a system of motor and cognitive skill development within an enjoyable, warm environment which includes play and creative activities. The records kept on the progress of children were used to help individuals develop skills which were found to be in need of strengthening. But throughout the year a process of interaction took place between members, at a group and at an individual level, in a very dynamic way.

But skill of reading is not the most important goal to be attained, for although it may open the doors to academic study, its use, in general terms, is diminished in modern technological society which uses the spoken word and visual images for communication, constantly and indiscriminately. The prime goal to be attained, mainly through the educational system, is the power to discern and make choices based on the consideration of all relevant factors. Concept development is implicit in these processes and yet children are expected to reach the level of formal operation, almost spontaneously. The lessons to be learnt from the interventionist programmes are: that children of a very young age have great potential but are frequently inhibited by the limited expectations of adults; that although individuals vary in rate of development and growth, with careful diagnosis, slowing development can be accelerated; that concepts can be taught with skill and understanding; that the early years require structure more than at any time in the child's development; that these processes are required by all children irrespective of the circumstances in which they are living.

A recurring theme in most programmes of intervention has been the need to enhance feelings of self-esteem in disadvantaged people. The sense of failure produced by the society in which they live has a powerful psychological effect of dominating proportions. Contributory factors such as poor housing, lack of work, physical illness, attitudes of professionals in helping and support agencies (including schools) produce a demoralized group of people. Consequently a number of programmes have attempted to develop a sense of identity among individuals and, in so doing, have highlighted a need for the whole population. It is becoming increasingly clear that a major function of the educational process is to enable self-identity to develop. Although it is not the function of this chapter to discuss the methods teachers in schools might use to help pupils to develop a sense of identity, particularly during the secondary stage of education, the process commences at birth. There is a close correlation between identity of self and conceptual development. Admittedly other powerful determinants also contribute, notably the relationship of parents to each other and to their child, but it is important for teachers and leaders in pre-school groups to be aware of their potential to assist the formation of identity in young children from all social backgrounds.

The danger in advocating a structured methodology in working with young children is that 'structure' can be interpreted as a closely controlled, narrowly defined series of detailed stages or lessons to be presented to an unsuspecting group of innocents. In the terms of this discussion 'structure' should be seen rather as a series of challenges presented to a child by a teacher who possesses sufficient information to allow a fair prediction of the child's success in meeting those challenges. If this process is carried out in the presence of the child's mother or father in order that they, too, should understand the way in which their child is developing intellectually, a very positive interaction can begin. Not only is the learning momentum maintained, but the parents can begin to see the differential rates in growth of other children in the group, not in terms of a competitive movement but as a perfectly normal process. In other words, the teacher is able to ease the pressure exerted by anxious or ambitious parents on their children and is able to encourage less self-assured parents in their role as educators of their children.

Implications for the parents of young children

The parents' role in the total development of their child has overriding importance beside other contributory factors. Their love and concern, their ability to communicate, their ability to provide, their ability to protect, during the very early period in the child's life, has a profound effect in his later development. The emotional and physical state of the parents, particularly of the mother, has a marked effect on the family. Many children who behave in a disturbed way in school and in the community are manifesting the disturbance of their parents.

The need for pre-schooling to be seen as an extension of family life is becoming widely recognized. The reinforcement of this view on a large scale is being established in practice by the Pre-school Playgroups Association and other voluntary bodies. Research studies, as described previously, have been designed to show the parents their potential in teaching language and cognitive skills to their children. In many families this process happens almost unconsciously as mothers reinforce the understanding of their children constantly through everyday occurrences in their homes. The mother who responds to a child's question with a descriptive sentence or perhaps another question, contributes to a perceptible increase in the child's verbal ability and his understanding of meaning. She may also find that she is learning from her child as she discovers facets in the unfolding process of growth which are displayed as her child develops. Motivation for learning, in this sense, is high, since it is her child she is discovering.

The powerful motivation provided in a mother–child, father–child learning situation has been recognized in some of the early education programmes previously described. In many of such situations, when a teacher is present, to form what might be called a 'triumvirate of learning',[30] it is difficult to isolate pre-school education from adult education. Indeed future educational policy may well recognize the need for such joint provision. Peri-natal programmes are being suggested as a method of giving advice on the parents' part in the intellectual development of their babies from birth onwards to complement advice and help more generally provided by the health service. Pilot programmes, such as the Thomas Coram Nursery sponsored by Thomas Coram Foundation and, again, at Red House, are pioneering work in this field. Attempts are being made not only to study the mother–child relationship in an educational context but also the father–child relationship, which is much more tenuous and delicate to interpret in intra-familial terms. Such programmes can only marginally affect mothers who for economic or social reasons, need to work. Ideas which use the established principle of 'day-release', to provide mother-child groups in areas of high female employment, are being canvassed. But the national economic climate is a strong determinant in encouraging and sustaining such ideas.

It has been suggested that children born during the period of the First World War produced a second generation of children during the Second World War, who were a noticeably deviant group throughout their educational careers. The cause of deviance is suggested to have originated in disturbed parent–child relationships during the early years of the children's lives. It is possible that periods of economic acceleration which demand high female employment may also be measurable later in terms of an increase in unsettled behaviour in children. It follows therefore that nursery education which enables an increase in the employment of mothers to occur, would be rendering a grave disservice to future generations. Clearly the nursery which depends upon mother and father participation in order that the educational processes set out in this book, may occur, is contributing to the life of the community in a very positive way. The greatest hope for schools to grow as community resources, in which parents and teachers can be identified as joint contributors to the development of children, lies in the nursery movement. Equally such hopes could be dashed if misunderstanding and professional ethics help to perpetuate the present compartmentalized, or 'egg-crate', structure[31] of the educational system, through the nursery schools. The trump card is in the hands of parents, however; nursery and playgroup provision is an option which they may accept or reject.

5

Networks for learning: educative processes within the community

A perspective which views the child and its psychological development as a centre of interest is avoiding important areas which have great relevance for early education programmes. We have shown in the case study contained in Chapter 3 that the reactions and developmental growth of a child can have a profound effect upon its parents. Just as the child is the product of a genetic heritage and of a particular environmental climate, so will its awareness of family and surroundings produce changes in the family. At an obvious, and basic, level this may be provision of furniture and space for an additional member of the family in their home or a rearrangement of the parents' times of sleeping to come to terms with the new child's demands for food. Equally obvious is the effect upon the next day's work and relationships when the parents have a a sleepless night caring for a child who is fractious and unsettled. The child in the family exists in a sociological dimension which is important not only within the home, but also within the area of the family's influence and interaction. Our case study described a family-centred approach to early education and outlined the processes of communication and development which were possible in a pre-school group. We have suggested that through the influence of children regularly meeting together to play and develop in an environment for group learning, the parents themselves are affected by the process, especially when their role as educators is emphasized.

In this chapter we turn to the influences early education programmes may have on a wider basis and consider the human and environmental factors from its surroundings which will affect the operation of a pre-school group.

Educationists have for some years been concerned with the relationship between schools and their communities and the growth during the early 1970s of community schools both in Britain and in other countries, reflects a growing realization that life outside school walls cannot be ignored. Early education programmes commence with a head start over established schools. There is no statutory obligation for parents to take, or send, under-fives to nursery classes or playgroups. Where the invitation exists from teachers and group leaders for parents to stay with their children in group activities or where home-visiting schemes are taking place, a closer community contact has already been established.

Some readers will feel that the question of defining the concept of community has been begged; it must indeed be admitted that it is not a precise sociological concept and has been used rather as a generic term, in this and probably other writings in the field, to indicate associations of individuals who can be grouped in a variety of ways for a variety of purposes. The fact that there may be no single common defining characteristic does not itself invalidate the concept, nor prevent it having meaning for the individuals so classified. It may not always be possible for an individual to identify a set of primary and secondary relationships which form his neighbourhood or community grouping, or he may identify such a grouping or network of groupings but be unable to locate himself within it. None of these conceptual difficulties negates the usefulness of words like community or neighbourhood, and surely cannot destroy the commonsense notion that social processes and services occur on a local basis to aggregates of people. A common situation in local affairs and institutions is for these aggregates to be formed differently for each function; and yet even where the regrouping is more than marginal, overlaps between the various spheres of communal life will still be large and significant. The local sphere of influence enjoyed by the educational system is more clear than in the case of many institutions; one could argue that it is, if anything, too formally delineated.

Since we are concerned with the development of provision for the under-fives, which will be fused to the educational system, a definition of 'community' can be made in geographical terms. Catchment areas of schools cover neighbourhoods which can easily be identified. A collectivity of neighbourhoods would, for our purposes, constitute a community.

While not attempting a wider definition of the term, there are theoretical considerations which have a bearing on the general theme of this chapter. Immediate problems present themselves when considering the word 'community'. In spite of common usage, community remains a confusing, untidy and difficult term. Vague phrases such as 'the world community' or 'the community sentiment', more often confuse than clarify. The changing nature of the concept of community adds to the difficulty.

R.M. MacIver's definition[1] which he wrote in 1917, reflects the changes which have taken place in theories of social organization.

> By a community I mean any area of common life, village or town or district or country or even wider area. To deserve the name community the area must somehow be distinguished from further areas, the common life may have some characteristic of its own such that the frontiers of the area have some meaning. A community is a focus of social life, the common living of social beings.

He proceeds, in his definition, to widen this view. 'Community is no greater mind, but it is created by that activity of men's minds in which they relate themselves incessantly to one another.' He is therefore producing from an earlier concept of static village life, the notion that community is a fluid situation. This view is supported and developed by G. H. Mead[2] who recognizes that it is the organized community or social group which gives to the individual his unity of self, termed 'the generalized other'. Mead states that social and group attitudes are brought within the individual's field of direct experience and are included in the structure of his self. Thus self becomes an individual reflection of the general systematic pattern of social and group behaviour. A discussion of community therefore evokes considerations of identity, of commitment, processes of interaction such as communication and the handling of conflict, tensions between the person and the larger whole. A necessary part of this discussion must be an examination of the collectivities which may contribute towards a notion of community within a modern urban society. A. O'Brien[3] sets the scene well:

> We are all living together, travelling further, meeting more people. We do not move along parallel lines like trams but continue to criss-cross each other's tracks like taxis. We tread on each other to reach the same dung like puppies. We coagulate like nests of bees. And we are not free-falling through space but obey, whether we like it or not, the universal pull of social gravity, the tidal currents of communal conformity, towards the same places, the same jobs, the same entertainments, the same wives, the same routines.

This description implies that although the boundaries of community may no longer be clearly defined, groups exist which contain structure. Berger and Luckmann[4] give a clear account of the way humans create structures in order to facilitate interaction. At the same time they describe the way such interactions become institutionalized through habitualized actions and, over a process of time, produce situations from which it is difficult to break out. The gains which Berger and Luckmann claim are made are that the individuals concerned in the process of institutionalization are able to predict each other's actions and the interaction of both becomes predictable.

> They save time and effort, not only in any external tasks they may be engaged in, separately or jointly, but also in terms of their respective psychological economies. Their life together is now defined by a widening sphere of 'taken-for-granted' routines. Many actions are possible on a low level of attention. Each action of one is no longer a source of astonishment to the other.

Within such institutionalized activities members of the community may receive security and comfort. The question still remains for community dwellers, 'How does man break out of this situation?' 'What is required to change the *status quo*?' Since the discussion claims so far that within urban communities mobility exists, the situation is fluid. One of the causes of such fluidity is conflict. Social structures within communities cause conflict. Georg Simmel suggests that a certain amount of discord and controversy is organically tied up with elements which hold individual groups together. He emphasizes that conflict is a necessary means of expression in order to establish identity and that it plays an important part in all human affairs. He dispels images of future communities living in total and complete harmony. An analysis of conflict shows that community disagreements may be used as a measure of community life. Issues change from specific disagreements to more general ones and then into new issues.[5]

Clearly conflict is related to power within communities and the topic will be discussed later with particular reference to education. For the moment, the power of the group to curtail the rights of the individual and the power of one community to dominate or influence others is a facet which is being felt forcibly by many people. Power must form an important component of any examination of collectivities forming communities. Durkheim[6] expresses the view that the development of power within a series of 'secondary groups' is a necessary element of conservatism through which a nation may be maintained. This view raises an interesting comparison between the need for conflict by individuals within the group and the need for conflict by groups within nations, in order to retain identity.

The individuals within the groups so far described are all, at the same time, members of families. It is possible to view community as an extension of the family or a larger kinship unit and indeed, even in modern urbanized society, such extensions of family still exist. But they are to be found where there is a close affiliation between a single major occupation of the work force and a community as in farming, or the fishing or mining industries. In spite of dramatic social changes in most societies the family is still an important agent in determining patterns of commitment. The ways in which families shape personal values and guide development ultimately influence the ways in which individuals create a private view of the wider social world. It is also true, however, that other socializing agencies, the school and peer groups, challenge the monopoly of the family, particularly as the structure of the family is weakened by other social influences such as increased mobility, poor housing, etc.

Organizations also play an important part in determining community. Work organizations form a particularly important part of many individuals' lives. Where many individuals form part of one work organization within a community, then the collectivity will exert considerable influence over the values and attitudes of that community. However, this is not the norm for most communities where many smaller work organizations may exist with little influence on each other apart from competition for individuals to form work forces. Such situations produce very limited loyalty to the work organizations and paradoxically lead to a fragmentation of loyalties to other organizations within the communities. This increased mobility of work forces may lead to a decreasing number of organizations concerned with social activities.

The study of organizations is complex, concerned with goals and social bonds as their principal variables. The structure of organizations may be studied without acknowledging the dynamics of individuals who form the organization. D. Silverman[7] argues for alternatives to the functionalist perspective which has dominated the study of organizations in recent years. His use of the word 'attachment' to describe membership in organizations provides a useful term to suggest the instrumental ties of person to organization without closing off the concept from the addition of more subjective and affective ties.

Within the organization cells or nodes comprising sets of intersecting relationships can occur to form social bonds. Social bonding is not concerned with the size of organizations, the members who make up the whole, but in the sharing of opportunities and experiences. The ideas of both 'bonding' and 'attachment' are seen as processes which are not fixed, since the view is taken that the interaction of the members of an organization can bring about change by the meanings that the members attach to their own and each other's acts.

The word 'community' then can be used in conjunction with social networks comprising intra-familial and extra-familial groups, short-lived temporary groups or organizations which adopt communal characteristics.[8] It is important to stress that in these collectivities a continuous process of definition and redefinition through the motivated interaction of individual members is taking place. Communication plays a vital part in this interaction and all collectivities have some recognized channels from which messages may be selected. John Dewey[9] summarizes the importance of communication.

> To learn to be human is to develop through the give and take of communication an effective sense of being an individually distinctive member of a community; one who understands the beliefs, desires and methods and who contributes to a further conversion of organic powers into human resources and values.

Situations for learning—a case study

It is possible to examine more closely, in a practical setting, some of the parts of the flexible changing webs of interaction so far described. The environment in view is a mining town of 17,000 people. In all, 3,000 of the children are attending full-time day school, and 58 per cent of the male working population are employed by the National Coal Board, many in the local pit which, with its attendant railway sidings, dominates the valley. The town is built on the north-east slopes of the Don Valley and consists of a mixture of late-Victorian housing stock built by the pit company, surrounded by estates of more recent houses, many owned by the National Coal Board, and much newer development by the local council. A large programme of rehousing families living in old 'two up, two down' houses is in progress. Throughout the town a number of pubs and clubs, clustered in three groups, are situated within easy reach of most people. The district council has a firm policy of providing special housing and centres for a growing number of retired people over the age of sixty-five. Resulting from this policy, three groups of bungalows have been built around centres staffed by full-time wardens. There are no large stores and the shops are all owned by local individuals; in addition, the market place opens each Friday. Nine fish-and-chip shops provide a seven-day service and a converted cinema is open similarly for Bingo players. Two youth clubs and five betting offices offer a limited six-day service. Four infant schools, six junior schools and one secondary school provide a limited five-day service. Two clinics operated by vastly over-worked health visitors and doctors (all of whom are Asiatic) attempt to meet the needs of an area which has one of the highest incidences of ill health in the country. The Roman Catholic Church with its complex of school, club, convent and presbytery, enjoys the continued support of many Roman Catholics in the town and is the envy of the Protestant churches which are declining sharply in numbers.

This is the frame of the picture which is being examined. Where are the 'webs of interaction'? What are the sources of learning? The pit, for instance, offers a powerful situation for learning. It has particular and peculiar geological characteristics, which can only be learnt by direct experience and if learnt badly may result in the death or serious injury of miners. The working faces are difficult, dangerous, unpleasant, noisy places for teams operating coal-cutters and it is at this point that the attitudes of the workmen to each other and to work are formed. Here, there must be total dependency upon each team member to carry out specific functions; here skills are formed, bitterness is engendered and young men are initiated. The results of such explosive, powerful learning are transmitted into other webs of interaction. Families are certain to be influenced by the attitudes of father and sons of working age. It is not surprising that many sons are actively discouraged from working in the pit by their fathers and that 'education' is seen as a means of escape for many.[10] Traditional attitudes towards husbands by wives play an important part in deciding the ways in which they will organize and run their domestic affairs. The shift system will condition, to some extent, attitudes to spare time and types of activities carried out by members of the family, but these tend to be centred around other collectivities such as clubs for shooting, pigeon and greyhound racing, and social activities.

Learning clearly takes place in club situations. Motivation to learn is high. If pigeons are to be trained to fly higher, faster, more accurately, then complex feeding, training and handling procedures need to be understood. Business procedures for organizing and running the clubs and races are learnt by aspiring committee men because they are motivated to do so. The same process of learning takes place, more systematically, with local union members who desire to play larger roles in their organization. Similarly members of social clubs who feel that they have a flair for efficient control of the bar takings may learn the process at the expense of the club. Throughout the club networks, however, apart from the obvious learning situations stated, a whole process of social interaction is carried out in a particular setting, still dominated to some extent by attitudes learnt in the pit, which enables a large number of people to develop skills which may loosely be termed 'social'. Similar skills may be developed on the street corner, in the pub or Bingo hall. In the latter situation, of course, it is possible to obvserve a further release of energized interaction where hopes and fears may be transmitted into fact or fiction by one incomplete line on a score card. Here cults and mysticisms may be formed and dissipated quickly as lucky seats, special coats, charms, secret invocations are tried and fail.

Bingo may form an escape from the difficulties of housekeeping and shopping but it is in the shops that a further powerful learning situation may be found. Learning to stretch a limited budget to meet rising prices, and comparing the value of goods on display, are lessons which housewives teach each other very effectively. Once more, motivation to learn is high and the webs of interaction occur swiftly, producing an oscillation in role from teacher to learner. In this context, washeterias provide an interesting setting for longer periods of conversation or reading magazines and here it is possible for the attendant to play a helping role, in excess of her defined duties.

The helping agencies clearly have a role which enables members of communities to learn. The point of contact when this may happen most easily is in ante-natal or post-natal clinics where motivation on the part of mothers is high, but the process of learning within a health context should occur whenever people visit for medical treatment. Social workers are trained to use skills which are often based on psycho-analysis. They, too, endeavour to enable clients to learn, but frequently clients' motivation is low and the response which social workers hope for does not materialize unless welfare benefits are involved in the treatment plans.

To sum up, the view being presented of learning situations occurring within this particular setting appears to be dominated by the pit but to encompass the family scene, social activities in clubs and pubs, Bingo halls, and betting offices, shops, the libraries, allotments, churches, clinics and other social agencies. Where, then, on this list should the official seats of learning come? Clearly schools play an important role in the development of young people. But what is their relative importance in terms of the development of individuals during their life-span?

We are suggesting that the family-centred approach to pre-school learning offers a realistic possibility to school and the community, enabling, on the one hand an extension of school influence in childhood and adulthood, on the other hand the culture of the community to be more clearly expressed in the school.

The possibilities for interaction between community and pre-school groups are fairly obvious. First, one can point out that the impact of a pre-school group which includes parents as partners in the realization of psychological aims is felt most directly outside the group by the siblings of the parents who attend. Younger brothers and sisters will be the chief beneficiaries, since they have generally yet to reach the stage in their development with which their parents have become familiar by belonging to the group. Hopefully, the awareness of developmental processes possessed by the parents will be more general than this, so that their treatment of older children and the educational stages which they are undergoing will also be positively influenced.

Second, those families in the group who are neighbours or acquaintances will surely have contact with each other and part of that contact may revolve around the shared experience of assuming an explicitly educational role in the pre-school group and of attaining an informed approach to the development of their children and others'. Where the pre-school has included group conversations about the problems of children's development, and perhaps even wider-ranging subjects, the possibilities for a localized group forming between neighbouring families with children of the same age will be greater.

Third, perhaps the most powerful form of influence which the pre-school group with high parental collaboration can wield upon the community is that which results from the creation of successive corps of parents who have practical experience in educating their own and others' children. Following parental collaboration in pre-school, the reception classes and perhaps the entire infant department can be the beneficiaries of whole intakes of children with parents aware of the approximate stages of development of infants. The children, too, will represent levels of development which, before the setting up of a pre-school group, the reception class teacher may not have had to consider; and, in diminishing degrees, the same will apply to the higher reaches of primary education. At the pre-school level, the specialisms which tend to exclude the parents' educational influence upon the child are at a minimum. Also at the entry into infant school parents are in the position of having had the major responsibility for their children's development for a number of years, which is not in the interests of parents, teachers or children to truncate abruptly at school entry.

Fourth, one should consider the roles of professional agencies in the community other than schools, and the relations which a pre-school group might have with them. These agencies include the social services, educational psychologists and welfare officers, and health visitors. Pre-school provision cannot be geared to schools alone. Education should be meshed into the social and political infra-structure of the community. Thus housing, welfare, health and transport services equally may require changes in approach which acknowledge and include members of the community in their management. This raises a further issue in our consideration of community interaction. Where, in fact, does power exist in a community?

Power within the community

The mining community described in the preceding section could be examined to identify sources of power within it. The legitimated sources held by the members of the district council, the management department of the local pit, the NUM representative and various management groups elected to run clubs and organizations by their members, may be clearly defined.

Less clearly identifiable to members of the community is the power of the county council in controlling schools. Head teachers are seen very frequently as the sources of power since they appear to have complete autonomy not only over the children but also over the staffs in their schools.

The police represent the legal power of the government quite clearly and maintain a large local constabulary. Violence is not unknown in the town and control by the police is matched with physical response by members of the community, thus a reasonable balance of power is maintained. The local social work team represent a further branch of statutory power vested in the local authority.

By far the greatest manifestation of power at an individual level, however, is demonstrated by the government each week in the form of supplementary benefits, pensions, unemployment benefits and many other grants and payments. One-fifth of the population are in receipt of benefits, most of which cannot be negotiated by applicants. It is in this grey area of confrontation that the officials who have responsibility for disbursing payments can use the mists of official language and ruling to demonstrate their ascendant position to applicants.

Looking more closely at the webs of interaction, it is possible to see a structure which is inter-familial within streets or blocks of flats. It is based to some extent on sharing between families. Often items of food, kitchen utensils, sometimes money are lent in the process of frequent visits by women to each other's houses. Here a complex support system is built up which is an effective counter to difficult living conditions and compensates for the tendency of adult males to spend a great deal of time out of the house. A power system can exist within the context of such a structure and it appears to be based on the efficiency of women in maintaining their households rather than on the status of their husbands. Many of the families have had a continuous record of existence in the town for fifty or sixty years at least, making the ties of the community strong. A steady stream of people leave the community, having used the educational system to break out, but the majority are strongly influenced by the power of the community itself. This power is difficult to describe but is concerned with a security which comes from known things and relationships. It produces a conservatism which is reflected throughout the community.

In part, of course, the conservatism of the community comes from its sharp sex-division. An industry which is as exclusively male as mining gives rise to a 'secret society'[11] of adult males. Husbands tend to devote spare time participating in activities which are for male groups. Wives stay at home, look after the children and prepare meals for husbands.

The sex-division of the community is clearly shown in betting and gambling. Betting offices are used exclusively by men, Bingo is played exclusively by women. Both situations, however, exert very considerable influences over the groups involved. During the miners' strike (unofficial) of 1972 when for a period many families had no income, a bookie was heard to say that his takings 'were down to £1,000 this week'.

In a sense this brief attempt to identify sources of power points to the way in which the *status quo* is maintained at an exposed (official) level and bears out Berger's theory of institutionalization.[12] This leads once more to the questions: how can change occur? Does 'education' have anything more to offer than an escape route? What are schools for? Has an experimental view of learning any validity in a society dominated by school-based curricula and a conservative power structure?

Developing the Philosophy of Conscientization

The case study used in this chapter may be said to limit the possibility of generalization from it; however, there may be points which are applicable in a wider sense. The picture so far produced has described the webs of interaction between groups of people which may be termed communities, but these groups may possess bonds sufficiently strong to form a larger community. Essentially, however, the identity of the groups depends upon the identity of individuals within the groups. Berger and Luckmann[13] trace the stages of awareness necessary for man to achieve identity. Paulo Freire[14] demonstrates in his programme of literacy for Brazilian villagers the process of 'conscientization' in which individuals are brought to a realization of their own potential and identity. Within Freire's programme are seen the strands of power, meaning and interaction referred to earlier in this chapter. The philosophy of conscientization is just as applicable within a technological urban society, however. To take Berger and Luckmann a little further, it is possible to say that as a man becomes aware of himself and his potential, so will he be able to contribute proportionally to his society.

It is the business of education to enable this process to function. Eventually a community must stand on its feet and rejuvenate its world.[15] Professional teachers become enablers in this process which brings individuals within the community to a state of conscientization so that the present unevenness of the split-level society (professionals on one level and consumers on the other) is reduced.

What then, are the 'implications' for the professionals? By its very nature this community-orientated socialization process cannot be seen as a compensatory mechanism, for this would imply the importation of externally-prescribed contents or methods; whereas the strength of neighbourhood schemes, as conceived in this volume, is in their bringing an indigenous approach to bear on local problems.

The role of the locally-based professional, doctor, teacher, social worker, health visitor, policeman, probation officer, psychologist and adviser in the community is potentially dependent on the fact that they are all working approximately the same 'patch'. Their collaboration can be very simply engineered but there are dangers to be avoided in the too free circulation of confidential information about cases, lest these individuals, who may already be experiencing some form of difficulty, are further weighed down and possibly discriminated against because of the existence of a large body of professional opinion about the nature of their case.

The fact that the professional's training may be acquired away from the community served does not imply that externally prescribed values need extend beyond the technical realm. Given an acceptable standard of technical competence, a reasonable ethic for the professional working in the community would be to enable individual and neighbourhood values full play.

The pre-school group provides the chance for the teacher to identify individual and neighbourhood values in her contact with parents day by day. It is possible for the learning processes seen in a small child to become a source of excitement and motivation to learn on the part of parents. Equally, the responses of parents can be of great value to the teacher.

A family-centred pre-school group operating effectively within a community could radically change the traditional role of a nursery class teacher in a number of ways, which involve, for instance:

1 Making a series of visits to invite children to attend the group with their parents. Home visits would be made during succeeding weeks to ensure that parents understood the objectives of the group's activities.

2 Seeing the mother, even though she may be living in a depressed state, as an equal partner in the process of helping her child to develop.

3 Accepting that the mother will know far more about the growth and development of her child than the teacher.

4 Within the group, looking for ways of maintaining the momentum of activities in the homes of the children.

5 Being prepared to place some responsibility for learning situations within the group upon parents.

6 Looking for skills in the parent's group and using her own skills and techniques in a complementary way.

7 Working at different levels at any time during group sessions, i.e. working with an individual or group of children at one moment, moving to an adult teaching situation during the next, holding a seminar for adolescent helpers at the end of a session, but all the time coping with the daily demands of the nursery class.

8 Channelling the energies of a parent group, who may be inclined to act collectively in a negative way, into positive support for individual parents who may be undergoing stress at home.

The usual procedures of record-keeping, organization of stock, layout of the room, etc., remain as a part of the teacher's duties. It will be, therefore, that far from 'diluting' the professional's work in the classroom a higher degree of expertise, particularly in relationships and communication, is required. The competence of the teacher to work with the age group of children must necessarily be unquestionable.

Implications for individuals within the community

'Adults must learn to confront an uninvented and undiscovered present.' Paul Goodman's comment gives a clue to objectives of early education, except that the whole age range of the community could be included. But it is easy to write cleverly constructed statements for the benefit of mankind without involving mankind at all. How can individuals achieve the level of self-awareness described in this chapter?

Three factors which have a bearing on the level of self-awareness reached in an individual could be considered: role, webs of interaction and motivation. Roles may change as an individual moves from one web of interaction to another. She may be a mother preparing a meal for a family in one setting but a secretary in an office in another and a member of a dramatic society in a third. Such roles may be sharply defined, but her degree of self-awareness in any of them may be inconsistent. It is probable that her motivation as a mother is greater than in the other two roles, but that her level of awareness is greater in her role as a member of a dramatic society since she is forced to project her conscious reality into different and unknown spheres.

Education should offer individuals opportunities to project their conscious reality into different and unknown spheres. This can only be achieved if motivation to do so is present; thus an adolescent who wishes to know more about ornithology may be able to identify birds well, but requires the stimulus of another ornithologist's presence and expertise in order to move into a different level of self-awareness. As his level of awareness increases, so is his morale being enhanced. His potential as a person and in the community, is widened.

The mother who has a young family in a downtown suburb may see her role forcibly as a provider of food and comfort for her children, but it is possible for her to enter a new role as an educator of her children with the guidance of a teacher who herself has adopted a new role. This role takes the teacher into the home of the mother and encourages a partnership in the process of helping the intellectual, as well as the emotional and physical development, of the children in the family. Experience in this field is already showing changes in the rate of children's development, but also important changes in the mothers' expectations and awareness. Interestingly, the process of educational-visiting is leading to further webs of interaction within communities as parents form groups for discussion and action.

The claimant who joins a group formed of people receiving benefits may achieve a higher level of self-awareness when, armed with greater knowledge of the benefits system, he confronts the supplementary benefits officer and wins his case. To carry out this process, however, he must move from the role of a conforming beneficiary into an advocate of a cause.

In varying degrees each of the situations described implies a shift of power. Without such a shift of power, the liberalizing effect of education cannot occur. This perspective of community education is not implying, however, a general revolution leading to an anarchical situation; rather it follows the implications of Freire's notion of a dialectic between the haves and have nots.

Also implicit in this perspective of community education is a recurrent or continuous process which first recognizes the way a community as a whole learns, generates energy and develops, then responds to individual motivation and needs. This means that the webs of interaction, as a phenomenon, must be recognized and sensitive support given in the form of ideas and expertise, if it is required.

Schools play an important part in the process of community education whether or not they are in tune with the particular attributes and deficiencies of people in their local areas. Within them children learn and develop skills in a particular way which would be otherwise impossible. They offer their pupils a cultural heritage which is national in scale. They are a window on the world, bringing ideas from beyond the community, knowledge belonging to many disciplines and the creativity of a host of peoples. Their organizational system reflects that of society, and regulations for the good, or safety, of the school community instil a concept of order and self-discipline in future citizens. Schools represent a specialized form of intervention and their presence is a reminder that change will not necessarily happen spontaneously. Influences and resources which enable change to occur more readily are a basic requirement. Whether schools have succeeded, or failed, to act as agents for change with local communities or wider society, is not the direct concern of this book. A growing library of literature on the need for alternatives in the educational system or the need to de-school society reflects the concern of some educationists for the future.

Our thesis accepts that a school system is an existing fact and is expanding slowly to include a wider age range. Our concern is that the lower edge of the expansion becomes defined less as an escarpment between the community and the schools, but rather as a blending which is extremely sensitive to local strengths and weaknesses. The growth of early education programmes provides an opportunity for merging which has not occurred before in the history of education. Paradoxically, the heritage of a century of public education has been to create a demand for more. Perhaps the supply of more education to a new, younger population will acknowledge the tremendous potential of parents and so create a new climate for change.

6

New directions in early education

One of the paradoxes of systems which depend upon economics is that expansion is not related to inflation, they are unhappy bed-fellows. *A Framework for Expansion* was followed almost immediately by a period of accelerating inflation which has caused grave problems for local government administrators who have been confronted with planning priorities on a shrinking effective budget. Such problems have had the effect of restraining developments in education which have outcomes difficult to predict. Early education experiments have produced ideas which are more radical and diverse in their strategies than most other sectors of the educational system. Expansion of ideas is not necessarily incompatible with economic recession. However, in spite of financial limitations, imaginative schemes have commenced in some areas. The results of such schemes are gradually being published and this chapter examines some of them as alternatives to the more usual playgroup or nursery-class provision.

Educational home-visiting

The educational-visitor programme at Red House, described in Chapter 3, coincided, during the final year of its operation, with the appointment of a number of teachers in the West Riding LEA to carry out similar work. In Birmingham, the Priority Area Playgroups Project appointed four visitors to work with the housebound parents and their pre-school-aged children. At the same time the City of Lincoln LEA appointed a visitor to work with children who were about to enter the St Giles Nursery School. Following these appointments during 1973 and 1974, a small, but increasing, number of educational-visitors have been appointed to work in areas of social disadvantage.

A survey[2] has been carried out from Southampton University during the first year's operation of fifteen educational-visitors who have been pioneering the work of home-visiting in England. While the results of the survey are still being assessed at the time of writing, it is already clear from the evidence available that the strategy has been tried under a variety of social conditions which are very different from those in the original area of the home-visiting experiment. Interestingly, although one or two schemes have followed the Red House model closely, the rest have adopted a number of diversified approaches to suit local conditions. Clearly, areas which contain a high proportion of Asian families will present different situations to the educational-visitors than a coal-mining town or a rural area. The spectrum of social conditions presented in the survey has provided a colourful backcloth against which to examine the working of the strategy in a fairly rigorous way.

Common to all the schemes has been the principle of a weekly visit, usually lasting one hour, to the home of a family containing a child who, within a period of four to twelve months, will enter a nursery or reception class in the area. In this way, it has been possible for the visitors to demonstrate and articulate to parents that learning can take place in the home and involve those not able or willing to participate in a group.

The ages of the children visited has ranged from two to four years. Visitors have therefore developed various approaches suitable for different ages. They have taken books, materials, toys and equipment for the children to use during the weekly sessions and in many cases they have run a lending system of toys and books. In some areas severe language problems have been presented to the visitors when the parents, particularly mothers, have been unable to speak English. Language and communication have been important components of all the visiting schemes, not only directed at the children but also at the parents.

The parents have in fact been the prime object of the programme. If some knowledge of child development can be transmitted to the parents, the beneficiaries will include the whole family, particularly younger siblings; the schools and the community at large will also enjoy the services of informed adults.

The learning triad of child, parent and visitor is difficult to achieve in practice because of the conflicting demands on the time and concentration of the parent which are made by other children and domestic commitments. There has been a tendency for the visited family to treat the visitor as a confidante and informal social worker. The visitors have been quick to realize that mothers who are living under stressful family or social conditions require opportunities to talk out their difficulties. 'Parents as educators' become a meaningless cliché in such circumstances. A mother who is demoralized by her immediate problems finds great difficulty in turning her attention to the intellectual needs of her children.

The survey has shown many cases in which the educational-visitor has acted with great dedication as a front line for the professional social worker. However, two factors should be remembered about the strategy: first, the visiting is regular and is often spread over a period of one year; second, the family has the right to opt out of the scheme at a moment's notice. The schemes are primarily educational and in the majority of cases the visitors have been able to achieve a sensitive, but flexible, balance between the social and educational objectives of their work. Much has depended upon the way in which families have been selected for visiting. In some areas, selection has been based upon the Red House criteria of geographical location of the family, e.g. within a certain school catchment area, and age of the child being visited. Other areas have had families in social need referred for visiting, by social services, health or welfare departments and voluntary workers. One scheme has used the number of siblings in families as a criterion for selection.

Priority Area Playgroups, an independent organization, which works closely with statutory bodies in Birmingham, has a system of visiting referred families. The Project's educational-visitors include two qualified teachers, and two nursery nurses, led by an experienced market researcher, have proved extremely successful in reaching the educational and social objectives of their schemes. The majority of visitors in other areas have been qualified teachers appointed on a full-time basis to the staffs of nursery or infant schools to work with children who will form the next termly or yearly intake. The survey suggests that although teacher qualification is very useful, especially in relating to other staff members in school, other attributes are vitally necessary for visitors. 'They must be unbiased, non judgemental, able to work under any sort of conditions, knowledgeable without being dictatorial, helpful without being patronising, able to listen and sensitive to people's needs without appearing to probe into their private affairs.'[3] Above all, they must be committed to the work.

Educational-visiting is a demanding occupation. The conditions within some homes are far removed from those in a well-lit, warm, clean and ventilated classroom. The visitor is working in isolation and is vulnerable to the reactions of the neighbourhood. Often toys and equipment have to be carried into the homes when the weather is cold or wet. So what are the benefits of such a rigorous strategy?

Education is being taken to individual families, on their terms. They may accept or reject it. There is time to show parents, in a relaxed and, for them, secure atmosphere, their potential as educators of their children. The learning situation of the home can be widened as parent–child interaction is increased, reinforced by the visitor.

Links between helping agencies and schools can be strengthened when the roles of the educational-visitor and the social worker are mutually understood.

The parents' inhibitions about school can be reduced and the school staff may be more aware of home backgrounds and difficulties of families in their area.

The visitor can observe the intellectual growth of each child within the natural environment of his home.

The parents' and child's anxieties, as the time comes to enter school, can be alleviated, especially if the parents become a supportive part of the child's school life.

A parent's sense of isolation can be reduced by regular meetings with the visitor.

Individual visits to families very often develop into group meetings for parents, which, in turn, can lead to self-help activities within the community.

The educational-visitor survey has emphasized several key questions about the strategy which, in spite of its clear potential for change so far demonstrated, require consideration in future developments.

1 How much is educational-visiting an intrusion into family life?

2 How can the cultures of ethnic groups remain unaffected within a visiting programme?

3 How can a balance between the social and educational issues within family situations be maintained?

4 What is the most effective curriculum for individuals and how structured should it be?

5 What constitutes a reasonable work load for the visitor?

6 How can colleagues on a school staff be informed about the day-to-day running of the programme?

7 How closely do the local social workers liaise with the educational-visitor?

The first complete year of operation during 1973-4 has shown a very low number of families who have refused to take part in the schemes and only two have dropped out. All the visitors received a warm and supportive response from the families with whom they worked and found few relationship problems in their weekly sessions with the parents and children. Most claimed that very noticeable changes in levels of communication between the child and the parents had occurred over the past year. A number of visitors stated that the work had radically changed their professional approach to teaching, mainly through their observation of the child within his primary learning situation.

The strategy also had a considerable impact on two schools which previously had experienced difficulty in establishing good contacts with their local communities. In one, parents are responsible for running a playgroup on the school premises and are active members of a residents' association and a welfare club, joined by members of the school staff. In the other school, parents take part in meetings and filmshows and one mother is running a course in the local Pakistani dialect for members of the school staff.

In spite of a total of over 4,000 visits made during the year, it appears that little is known about the life-style and child-rearing practices of some ethnic groups in this country. The knowledge and experience gained by the first pioneer visitors is of considerable importance for the future training of teachers, particularly those who will be working with young children. The results of their work could be of a longer-term nature than most pre-school programmes, since the emphasis of the visiting schemes has been concerned with attitudinal changes in parents.

Critics of the strategy emphasize its costliness in terms of the ratio of teachers to children and the limited time spent with each child. The survey shows that many families contain other siblings at home, who also enjoy a direct contact with the visitor. In multi-occupied houses, children from other families are frequently present when the visitor calls. This means that a visitor normally visiting 15 children per week may work with 30 children and 20 adults per week. During sessions, of course, visitor–child interaction is far more extensive than would be possible in the classroom and the results of this interaction may be retained for longer periods if the parent participation in the triad of learning has been positive.

Working with the family in the isolation of its home has disadvantages. The strategy was originally introduced for children aged eighteen to twenty-four months, who would not be ready for group activities. Older children and their parents too, may require group sessions in order to help their development. On balance, however, educational visiting has already shown that it can contribute positively in situations which otherwise would inhibit children's development. Child-minded groups are already being visited in Birmingham in this way,[4] providing a good example of a service which ultimately will help the children in the care of the child-minders, as well as the more immediate relief it brings to the adults involved.

The strategy also has a potential for rural areas where small groups of children are isolated and problems of transportation and supervision are high. Another interesting development is the Home-Link Project at Netherley, Liverpool, where two educational-visitors are training community aides to visit other families within the area. This work follows, to some extent, the model of the Home Instruction Program for Pre-school Youngsters (HIPPY) in Tel Aviv, Israel.[5] All of the schemes mentioned in this section have a common attitude to learning. It is through situations which result in action by the child and its parent that learning takes place. Each situation during a visiting session will produce action which the teacher (visitor) interprets in order to introduce a further context for action. A set of construction straws introduced by the visitor to the child may result in the child blowing through one of the straws and eventually discovering that the other straws will move if the air stream is directed at or near them. The idea of movement could be developed by blowing bubbles, rolling marbles, pushing model cars, etc., introduced by the visitor in response to the initial situation.

If the mother or father is observing the first situation and the teacher discusses possible subsequent situations, the triad of learning has commenced. Reinforcement of the parents' learning takes place when they introduce subsequent situations of their own interpretation. It will be seen that this process is simply an extension of the learning process which occurs naturally in any home situation. The visitor acts as a guide to open up new possibilities for learning which otherwise may not occur, and in so doing, learns herself about, and from, the family's responses.

'Home-start'

Family responses form an important part of a programme developed in

Leicester by Margaret Harrison.[6] As in the educational-visitor schemes, Home-start places an emphasis on educating both the parent and child together before formal schooling begins. Based on experience gained in the Demonstration and Research Center for Early Education (DARCEE) at George Peabody College, Nashville, Tennessee, and the Chicago Committee of Urban Opportunity, the programme uses a group of volunteers who visit two or three families each on a weekly basis. The programme is sponsored by the Leicester Council of Social Service and funded through an Urban Programme Grant for the period 1973-8.

The objectives of Home-start are:

1 To support and encourage mothers with their pre-school children and show them how it is they who can help their children to learn and develop their many potentials so that ultimately they may lead fuller and happier lives.

2 To work with any families who are experiencing frustrations or difficulties with their pre-school children, or even simply where a parent is in need of support and encouragement. (The Urban Aid Grant has been given to Home-start as it is seen as being a possible way of tackling the 'Cycle of Deprivation'. Therefore, although we are mainly committed to working with families who are referred by social workers, health visitors, or the Family Service Unit, nevertheless we would not exclude self-referrals.)

3 To use volunteers for the Home-start visits. In a 'Mum-to-Mum' relationship, one mother can share her time, concern and skills with another, thus representing a caring community, while at the same time doing useful preventive work, which social workers and health visitors, who are already over-burdened, can never hope to undertake alone. Home-start is developmental rather than remedial.

4 To build on the parent as the 'sustaining agent' in the child's life and to build on the home as the 'sustaining background'. Thus a Home-start volunteer can offer an individual programme to suit the needs of a particular family, helping the parents and children to develop their skills and attitudes and to maximize the effective use of the space and materials available to them.

5 To concentrate on the use of low-cost or no-cost materials available in even the poorest homes and to show the parent how she can turn everyday activities and tasks into tools of teaching. (Home-start volunteers are, however, able to borrow good and often expensive items from the Red Cross Toy Library for their families to use, suitable for the developmental stage and needs of each child in a family. Eventually, as the Home-start volunteer withdraws, the parents themselves will be introduced to the Toy Library, so that they can continue to avail themselves of the toys and equipment available.)

6 To keep the cost of the scheme to a minimum, by using volunteers for the actual visiting; by working in the homes, rather than running an expensive Centre; and as has already been stated, by using low-cost or no-cost toys and equipment.

7 To focus on the parent rather than on the child. Thus the parent is

encouraged to realize her worth as the 'expert' for her own child, and if an hour or so every week is to have a lasting effect, then the parent is the best possible person to sustain any progress made.

8 To build the parent's self-confidence, not only so that she is better able to cope with her pre-school children, but that her new competence has its effects on other family members and indeed on her interaction within the community.

9 By working with and through the mother, the Home-start volunteers' objectives in the course of a series of visits are:

to encourage physical contact between mother and child;
to encourage verbal contact between mother and child;
to encourage the child's language development;
to encourage sensory stimulation;
to encourage play;
to encourage the mother to use positive reinforcement;
to encourage independence (a) of the child–so that he learns to do things for himself by himself; (b) of the parent–so that she learns to do things and think of activities for her child by herself;
to encourage self-respect–so that both the mother and child feel that they CAN DO things;
to encourage outings locally with the child;
to encourage the use of community resources.

10 By working with and through the mothers, the Home-start volunteers aim to promote the overall development of the children:

physically, how they use their bodies;
emotionally, how they feel about themselves and others;
socially, how they relate to others;
and intellectually, that they learn how to learn.

Thus it is hoped that mothers will learn to provide stimulation and experiences which are appropriate to the child's developmental level, and which enhance the child's perceptual, conceptual and linguistic skills, as well as fostering persistence, positive self-esteem, independence, the desire to achieve, the ability to delay self-gratification and ultimately to develop a positive attitude towards school.

The volunteers have received a ten-week preparation course in (1) an understanding of relationships, (2) a knowledge of resources in the community, (3) child development, (4) the social work approach. The course has provided a foundation for their subsequent work with families during which the programme organizer has arranged support group meetings to discuss particular cases.

The strength of the programme lies in the impressive and careful way volunteers have been recruited, prepared for visiting work and provided with supervision. The team of ten Home-start volunteers (HSVs) and their organizer have generated a sense of cohesion which does much to overcome the isolation seen in the educational-visitor schemes where some visitors have felt very unsupported in their work.

Families to be visited are referred by social workers, the child guidance clinic, health visitors and community workers. A variety of referrals have been accepted, ranging from an affluent middle-class family to low-income, poorly-housed unsupported mother. Some have been visited for short periods of a few weeks, others for periods of up to one year. An important feature of the programme lies in the 'matching' of HSVs to the needs of families. The personality attributes of an individual HSV play an important part in deciding who will work with a particular referred family.

As was found in the experience of the educational-visitors, the Home-start volunteers' initial visits were often concerned with boosting the mother's confidence before she could turn to the task of stimulating and meeting the emotional and intellectual needs of her own children. Most of the volunteers have gained immediate acceptance, often because of what the programme organizer calls the 'mum to mum relationship'. This has meant that on occasions the HSVs have helped to relieve a family crisis by acting as a baby-sitter while a problem was resolved or taking a mother to visit her child in hospital.

A further important feature of the programme is the regular meeting of volunteers with the referring agents. This has resulted in a very positive relationship between the Home-start team and the various agencies who see the volunteers' work as a very valuable supporting and complementary part of social service. No doubt the sponsorship of Home-start by the Council of Social Service has enabled the programme to be accepted easily by professionals in the helping agencies, but much depended upon the sensitive, careful design and introduction used by the organizer.

From a community education viewpoint, the use of local volunteers who can identify with families in the neighbourhood is very desirable. The work however is demanding and requires, in some cases, long-term regular visiting. Whether the paid professional or the unpaid trained volunteer provides a more efficient service is not an issue in this programme. Much depends upon the continued understanding and support one group gives to the other. In the words of the organizer, Margaret Harrison,

> Home-Start so far is proving both purposeful and challenging, and, though only time will prove its true worth, great encouragement is derived from the positive initial reactions, both from the referring agents and the families themselves.[7]

The Playbus—education on the move

One of the most imaginative solutions in recent years to a local problem of pre-school provision was Dr Eric Midwinter's idea of taking education to the people by bus. He gives a graphic account of the growth and fruition of the idea in *Priority Education.*[8] Playbuses have been used in a number of urban areas since 1969, when the Liverpool version was first introduced, with immediate success, in the Bronte area of the city.

Initially, the converted bus was seen as a means of providing accommodation for pre-school group activities, where previously there was none. It was quickly realized by the Liverpool EPA Project team, that the Playbus was more than an immediate compromise solution. The process of its conversion, from a retired 'double-decker' bus to a schoolroom on wheels, by a group of lads in a local comprehensive school workshop, was a splendid example of community education. But when the schoolroom appeared on the streets in its new livery, children and mothers came on board and wanted to take part in the activities offered, because the appeal being made was dramatic and understandable. The Playbus was a 'barker for custom', enabling the need for pre-school groups to be spelt out to the administrators, while providing an opportunity for local families to demonstrate their desire to take part in an early education programme. Furthermore it represented a clear demonstration of the willingness of a group of educationists in the EPA Project to step over the school fence and take education to the doors of the community.

Well over thirty Playbuses are now operating in the United Kingdom[9] and as they appear at their daily stopping points to allow groups of fifteen to twenty children to play, discover and learn in a safe, attractive environment they spell out a message of encouragement to communities. It has been argued that the buses are expensive to run with rising fuel costs, wages for drivers and staff; that the vehicles depreciate rapidly, are difficult to heat and ventilate and that problems are present through lack of toilets, etc. These are considerable but probably surmountable obstacles. They are far outweighed by the possibilities for community involvement in pre-schooling which the Playbuses have encouraged. Playgroups have been set up and run by mothers following their initial experience in the Playbus groups. There is a potential and largely unmet need for Playbuses to be used in conjunction with child-minded groups, to help train the child-minders and to bring materials and equipment where needed.

Child-minded groups

It may seem odd to the reader that child-minding should be considered as 'pre-school activity' in this chapter. It may seem even stranger to combine it with imaginative or alternative methods of pre-schooling. It cannot be ignored. According to Brian Jackson's estimate,[10] between 100,000 and 200,000 children, mostly of pre-school age and a proportion of school-age, are in the care of child-minders while their parents are at work. Many of the children are in the care of 'illegal' minders who are not registered with their local social service department. There may be many reasons for non-registration. One of the commonest is that the premises are inadequate and do not contain suitable toilets. Jackson's graphic description of the conditions under which a large number of children spend many hours—far longer than the usual pre-school session—is moving and disturbing.

At the time of writing little positive help has been given to the minders, but in Birmingham, as mentioned earlier, one visitor has been appointed by Priority Area Playgroups to work specifically with child-minded groups.

Her first task was to find the groups. In an area where houses are occupied by several families this was not easy. In fact she found it impossible to trace any illegal groups although she knew they existed in the area. Each week the visitor calls on nine child-minders. She plays with the children, who range in age from a few months to five years, and introduces toys and equipment. When the minders realized that she was not selling the toys, but was prepared to stay and work with the children, they accepted her warmly.

The children often spend all day in a bare, cheerless room with few toys or games. The minder is carrying out a demanding job of feeding and washing a group of children for up to twelve hours. The appearance of a visitor with diversionary toys and equipment is a welcome break for all concerned. But it is relatively brief. Two hours each week has a limited effect on the children, but they clearly look forward to the day when 'the lady with the books comes in'.

The visitor feels strongly that registered child-minders should receive a small grant for toys and books and that if a positive rather than a critical view were taken by local authorities there would be a lower number of unregistered groups in existence.

A combination of a Playbus and a visitor working in areas where there are child-minded groups may be a way of enlightening and helping a group of women who, however rudimentarily, are providing a service. At the same time, such a combination would allow a considerable number of children to develop in a more enriched environment.

Multi-disciplinary centres

The problem of caring for children whose parents are both working or for other reasons unable to care for them during the day, has been faced for many years by the provision of day-care centres. As mentioned in Chapter 4 these cater for a very small proportion of children who require them. At the time of writing 20,000 places are available, often for the children of single-parent families, under the direct responsibility of social service departments.

Attempts are being made to combine the day-care emphasis of such nurseries with the educational emphasis of nurseries run by local education authorities. The Hillfields Nursery Centre has operated successfully since 1972 in Coventry.[11] It combines the two types of provision within one building by using staff who work in shifts (the Centre opens at 7.30 a.m. and closes at 6.00 p.m.) under the direction of a headmistress. Social workers whose case-load includes children attending the nursery liaise closely with the staff, thus providing a very positive demonstration of joint working between departments.

Such provision is not cheap. Facilities are required for preparing meals, accommodating and sleeping children from six months of age; staff trained in child-care are necessary in a high ratio of adults to children. The building is used continuously over a much longer period, however, and in terms of plant usage, the cost per building is rather less expensive than a nursery unit built to accommodate a group of thirty children for 1,200 hours per year. The Hillfields Centre, for instance, is open for at least four times this figure.

In Brunswick Square, London, the Thomas Coram Foundation has provided a centre[12] which has a wider provision. Here members of the Centre for Child Development form part of a multi-disciplinary staff who care for the needs of children aged fourteen months to four years. The children live in a nearby catchment area and include many referred by social workers. The Centre combines educational, day-care and medical services and is led by a head teacher. Great emphasis is placed on trying to respond to the needs of local families rather than organizing a slick, efficient, caring machine. The results of work at the Thomas Coram Centre are being monitored by a research staff and should contribute greatly to current knowledge of child development, as well as providing a detailed study of the idiosyncrasies of people from differing disciplines, who are drawn together in a common project.

A small number of similar centres are being considered at the time of writing. The Mulberry Tree Dorothy Gardener Centre, in Paddington, represents a further project to combine medical, social and educational provision for pre-school-aged children from an immediate catchment area. Such centres have provision for parents to meet for social or educational reasons and are intended to become foci for families containing young children in the local community. Much care is being given in setting up the Centre to the responses of local families to types of pre-schooling. It is their centre, not an experimental centre for the benefit of a University department.

Special centres

Much current thinking on community education, community medicine and community action stresses the need to use the mood, resources, environment of the local community to resolve problems and build up a sense of self-realization. The notion that members of a community with special needs should be treated in isolation does not fit current fashion. In practical terms however there is a major obstacle to these theories. Community action usually implies the presence of one or more people who work in a catalytic way to foster ideas and encourage groups to respond to situations confidently. Such work requires particular skills which are usually learned doing the job. Invariably reports of community projects stress the need for interdisciplinary understanding between professionals working in particular areas.

The Center for Preschool Services in Special Education, directed by Dr Louise Sandler in Philadelphia, has been successful in providing a diagnostic/therapeutic service for handicapped children aged from 36 to 63 months.

Children are referred by their nursery teachers to the Center if they show symptoms of speech impairment, emotional disturbance, learning disablement or neurological impairment. The children all attend federally-funded, normal nursery classes in the Hahnemann district of the city.

A 'chicken and egg' situation arises since the nursery teachers need an understanding of the symptoms before the children can be referred. When the children arrive at the Center for their half-day therapy sessions, the staff of the Center require knowledge of the methods used in the child's normal nursery.

In addition to the diagnostic/therapeutic service, in-service training forms an integral part of the Center's work. Medical students, art therapy students, mental health technology students, psychology students and teachers of pre-school classes are assigned to the Center by their Administrative faculty during their training. The Director and her staff of two teachers, two assistant teachers, social worker, psychologist and research worker co-ordinate and run the activities with the children.

A comprehensive service is provided for the children and their families including:[13]

1 evaluation and consultation; psychiatric, psychological and educational;

2 social service evaluation and intervention;

3 medical services;

4 language and speech evaluation;

5 diagnostic/therapeutic nursery classroom;

6 art therapy;

7 direct guidance to teachers of the regular nursery classrooms;

8 referral services offered to the families.

A prime objective of the Center, which began operation in 1970, is to provide a model of a neighbourhood referral centre for children attending nursery classes. The process of this development is slow, since staff must follow a pattern of in-service training first, however four neighbourhood units are now operating in the city supported by educational, medical and social work departments.

There is a strong emphasis on preventive aspects of the Center's programme and a further objective is that the community of parents, educators and mental health professionals recognize that young children, who require sensitive professional intervention, are not necessarily profoundly disturbed or disruptive. Staff of the Center hold regular meetings with groups of parents, and professionals to put forward this view.

The success which the Center for Preschool Services has had in softening the barriers between professional groups is largely due to the dynamic and persistent work of Dr Sandler. She has had the required vision, professional background and humility to co-ordinate the efforts of many people for the benefit of families in downtown Philadelphia.

Co-ordination of staff whose training and status differ widely is a major issue in the development of centres such as have been mentioned so far. Dr Mia Pringle's article 'Total approach to under-fives'[14] outlines the need for centres which cater for family needs rather than providing a specialized service. She, too, refers to the problems of integrating the work of people with differing backgrounds in training with the activities of a centre which may be wide-ranging. The model of the Center for Preschool Services would suggest that the key to such problems lies in the appointment of directors who possess a rare combination of professional skill, human understanding and stamina.

Peri-natal programmes

The rapid increase in emphasis on parent-education, which has developed in this country during the past few years since the publication of the Plowden Report,[15] has led to the formation of parent groups who discuss and study the behaviour of their children. This idea is not new. Parent education has been organized since 1964 in some European countries, for example by the International Federation of Parent Education based in Paris.

In Britain work in this field has not yet reached a stage of formal organization, although the Pre-school Playgroups Association has a firm parent-education policy now and would represent a large number of parents, particularly mothers. Experimental work under the aegis of adult education programmes[16] is showing the need some parents have to obtain a relief from the isolation of urban life caused through living in high-rise flats, or from the loneliness of unsupported motherhood, etc. The aim of such groups is to restore shattered confidence, improve morale and indirectly help to alleviate family stress. Such work is not restricted to particular class boundaries. Pressures and stresses causing depression and anxiety are found in all strata of society.

At Red House Education Centre, which has operated a number of interrelated programmes since 1969, a group has been formed of women in various stages of pregnancy and some whose babies are a few weeks old. The members tend to remain in the group from three to six months around the period of the baby's birth. The group is led by a mother who is also a qualified teacher. They meet for one afternoon each week and discuss various aspects of family life and child-rearing. The prime objective of the work is to allow the group members to receive help for emotional shock of pregnancy and later to realize the implications, and potential, motherhood has for the child.

One of the interesting findings of the Educational-visitor survey[17] has been that some mothers have no concept of motherhood since they, as children, received no mothering. The peri-natal programme is an attempt to use a group-dynamic situation to help mothers, some of whom may be thus handicapped. One of the major difficulties of such work is in encouraging fathers to take part as well. In many areas of Britain traditional attitudes of parent–child relationship are well established, and the important part the father plays in the self-identity of even a very young baby, is largely ignored.

Abbatt Homeplay Service

The growth of interest in pre-schooling which has taken place in recent years has brought with it an increasing range of books, toys and equipment marketed by educational and other business firms. Some items and kits are sold to parents as methods of 'raising performance' or 'awareness' in children from a very early age. No attempt is made to help parents understand the danger of pressuring children to carry out the tasks set by such kits.

A scheme which, although unashamedly commercial, sets out to promote the potential use of its products, in child development terms, to parents, commenced in 1974. Using a refined version of catalogue selling, the company appoints local advisers who must be interested in child development. The advisers are trained by an area consultant, usually a qualified teacher, so that when materials and toys are sold to parents, methods of using them can be demonstrated. Suggestions about play with items to be found in the home and the value of play to young children may also be made.

The idea originated from an apparent difficulty which parents, in some areas, found when they tried to buy educational toys, paint, paper, brushes, etc. By using an agency-selling technique the company hope to make a limited range of goods more easily available. The adviser holds a small stock of toys and materials which are sold direct to customers for cash.

There is a danger that the methods taught by the consultant may suffer from a dilution by the time they reach the parents; however the keenness of the advisers and the speed with which ideas and materials can reach parents is impressive. In addition, the idea of self-help is not incompatible with current ideas on community development.

TV for parents and children

As a means of disseminating ideas to a wide audience, television has an immediacy and capability not available to other communications media. The pictures move, the commentary keeps pace and the viewer can identify with actors on the screen while in the security of his own home. With the immediacy, of course, comes transience. Not every picture, idea or statement is remembered. Viewing at home is subject to many distractions and interruptions, particularly in homes which contain young children.

There are now many programmes designed for children transmitted regularly by the BBC or ITV. The majority fall under the category of entertainment while the rest are broadcast during programme time for schools. Until 1974 there was a clear dividing line between education and entertainment. A further line separated adult from children's programmes.

Some programmes for young children were specifically designed to allow the mother to leave the child watching the television.

Under the executive production of Claire Chovil, the BBC decided to introduce a series called 'You and Me' during schools' programme time, specifically for parents and their pre-school-aged children, but which could also be used by nursery classes. Each week during term time three related programmes lasting twelve minutes are broadcast, to be watched by parents with their children. Talking points are introduced and parents are offered guidance in developing them. On Fridays the programmes use a special technique in which a parent and child carry out an activity to demonstrate its possible results to viewers. The parent and child are not actors, neither are they rehearsed in a sequence of actions. The procedure used is to set up a situation which has fairly well-defined parameters for the parent. She may be asked to talk about reflections which can be found in her kitchen and to explore possible reflective surfaces with her child. Much depends upon the skill of the production team, cameraman, sound and lighting technicians, to create a relaxed filming situation. The result of the films is a series of studies showing different parents and children from a number of areas responding in a refreshing way to situations found in their local environment. The topic used each week is developed differently in each of the three programmes, which can be followed in a handbook for parents covering the series.

Television, by itself, does not present an alternative form of early education but it can form a powerful resource particularly in language development. For older children 'Sesame Street', 'The Electric Company' and 'Mr Rogers'[18] are good examples of programmes which mix education and entertainment. The production budgets of these programmes are very much higher than 'You and Me', but they indicate a scale of possibility in future TV programmes for parents and children.

Résumé

We have attempted to present to the reader in this chapter a scan of possible approaches to early education, which differ from more established provision such as playgroups and nursery classes. In a field which is developing rapidly, the list of experimental strategies and projects continues to grow. The bibliography published by the US Office of Child Development, *Home-based Child Development Program Resources* (1973), provides a good example of the acceleration in ideas and programmes during recent years. We cannot claim to have reviewed all current work, therefore, but we have identified developments which have implications for communities containing families with small children.

Clearly there is no global methodology which emerges; the reverse, in fact, applies. Particular strategies are required for specific situations as they are identified by members of communities. Even the example of television broadcasts, at present carried on a national network, would be more valuable if they were based on regions using local dialects and environments.

Some strategies overlap or can be combined. Educational-visiting can easily form part of normal nursery provision. Playbus schemes can combine visiting in homes, with group activities for parents as well as children. Existing nursery schools could extend their range of service by including day-care provision.

However strongly we feel that the role of parents as educators of their children is supremely important, the fact remains that many children are left in the care of other adults during the day. Support for children in such care is a vital requirement and any consideration of future strategies in early education should include studies of the family centres which are beginning to operate in this country and elsewhere.

In the final analysis our case rests on methods which will enable members of families to reach their potential as contributing parts of their community. The diversity of methods portrayed in a small way here, hint at the wider possibilities if flexible management and funding allow 'tailor-made' programmes to develop as required. This raises questions of control and evaluation for funding agencies but more importantly it raises questions of control and evaluation at a local, community level. Who, in fact, should run such programmes?

If provision for the under-fives is to be community-orientated to include parents and other adults who receive professional guidance, then the objectives of local programmes may well include increasing the share of control and responsibility undertaken by lay people.

There are clear implications, to be seen in such objectives, for the training of future and existing professional workers. Not only will students in training require first-hand experience in working with adults as well as children in the community, but ways need to be examined of allowing a new balance of control to develop in local groups. Training therefore becomes a dialectic process which grows with the community movement.

Our earlier reference to the Center for Preschool Services in Special Education illustrates an initial stage in the training of professionals, during which they are exposed to the skills and reactions of each other in a practical situation. There would appear to be no short cuts in this process. As more situations are created which allow professionals from various disciplines to work together so more opportunities for students to take part will slowly become available.

A number of colleges of education now include a social work element in their courses which allow students to work in communities on placement with social service departments. Wentworth Castle College in Barnsley has commenced a community-orientated nursery course which enables students to receive first-hand experience in educational-visiting, as well as in other types of provision for the under-fives. The course contains elements of child development and family interaction which are set in particular environmental contexts.

An important feature of the Home-start Programme in Leicester is its method of providing an initial course which allows the volunteers to study a range of topics related to their work, followed by weekly support meetings to discuss and exchange experiences and thoughts. This is much nearer to a dialectic process of training and development. It is of course limited to a small-scale operation, but perhaps provides a clue to the direction in which development of schemes, and training of personnel, could go in the future.

If the local needs of families within communities are to be met in a flexible way then many situations will be presented to leaders of groups or home-visitors which will require a method of field support similar to supervision facilities used by social workers. A process of field support which allows those who are working with the under-fives to meet together regularly, can become a vital, on-going method of training. Such a process places an inherent reliance upon the actual experience of the participants and uses it to develop their own resources further.

In-service courses for serving teachers, particularly in family-centred early education procedures, require three main elements:

1 There should be time devoted to exploration of child and family needs, conducted on an individual basis by course members into home and community situations.

2 Study sessions to consider recent theories of family and child development.

3 A practical extrapolation from the previous two elements is then required, to include strategies for particular school areas, group techniques in creative and imaginative work, individual skill requirements and methods of diagnosis linked to knowledge gained from the work of professionals in other fields. The principle of building upon the experience of participating teachers is an important and central part of such in-service training.

The work of the Pre-school Playgroups Association in running training programmes for group leaders and parents, is a good example of the way a voluntary, and grassroots, organization can develop its own systems and methodology in order to raise general standards of operating playgroups throughout the country. The Association has its own field support system through area organizers who visit playgroups, offering help and advice, as well as arranging local training sessions.

Other voluntary bodies such as Save the Children Fund and National Children's Homes have also been able to support field work by an organizational structure of advisers; however in these and other voluntary bodies it has proved difficult to maintain playgroups in some urban areas without extra supervision and leadership. The Southwark Playgroup Project, which set up and ran six groups to examine response by the local community to pre-school provision found that the groups could not sustain their initial momentum over a very long period without additional help from outside.[19]

The results of the Southwark experiment support the argument for different strategies in areas where a more traditional approach to early education meets with limited success. Our experience with one playgroup organized and run by mothers in a working-class area suggests that a high involvement by a supporting agency is required to help sustain the group over a long period of time. In addition to the familiar demands of a playgroup on the leaders to meet costs for rent, helpers, equipment and heating, this particular playgroup used premises which were burnt out twice by vandals, endured the pressures caused by a local strike, while coping with the difficulties of a polluted environment which remained as a constant hazard for health and cleanliness.

People who are involved in supporting such groups require to do so in a way which is unpatronizing and uncondescending, but which can bring high-quality guidance to those who have requested it. There is an obvious source for such help for local groups, but once more an element of training is necessary for those providing the guidance. The school system could include teachers with a special responsibility for stimulating community playgroups in urban or rural areas. As with the educational-visitors, such a strategy would be able to use the established foundation of the educational system as well as helping to develop, over time, a self-sustaining movement within the community.

In this way the fusion may occur of the educational potential in the community, which is a collectivity of families, and the school. Hopefully, the process will encourage school curricula to become more socially relevant, and invite people in the community to participate in the cognitive, creative and social objectives of the school.

7
In conclusion

Where resources are scarce, their optimum allocation is of great importance, and may not be met by an equal sharing out of these resources. In early education, where resources are becoming increasingly scarce, the prime examples of differential allocation on a national scale are the additional finance and facilities in educational priority areas, and the siting of many nurseries created under the expansion programme in areas of need; in both examples, positive discrimination is conceived as a means of extending the right to educational resources.

In order to operate, a policy of positive discrimination requires information which will identify need and enable extra facilities to be directed accordingly. Research has contributed to such policies by revealing the types of circumstance and attitude often associated with educational failure and by enabling need to be viewed in terms of social or educational disadvantage. The habit of linking need for extra facilities with disadvantage is encouraged by the practice of allocating those facilities on the basis of an area or some other large unit; it is admittedly difficult to discriminate individually within what is essentially a group provision, quite apart from the risk of stigmatizing the individuals who would be singled out. What concerns us more than the size of the unit perceived to be in need is the treatment which the individual or group receives under the discriminatory policy; for the analysis of society according to which EPA schools are designated, or according to which nursery units are located, can be developed quite separately from the programme which it is intended to apply within the discriminated sector. What concerns us here is that the analysis of the social difficulties which children and their families face, so often forcibly determines the treatment they should receive under policies of compensation. The notion of compensation for disadvantage conveys the message that children's successful development requires that certain deficiencies in their parents or background culture be made good. More often than not the process of making good is designed exclusively in terms of the requirements of the professional educator. Our reasons for believing the compensatory approach to result from a misinterpretation of social and educational phenomena are argued fully in Part 1: in particular, we tried to suggest that poor educational progress, in so far as it is associated with social factors, may arise from cultural differences between teachers operating with established methods and curricula and families within whose life-styles such concepts are alien; it was not accurate, we argued, to regard underachievement as a result of a deficiency on the part of only one side in the socializing partnership of home and school, or pre-school. There is, to follow up that line of thought, a more practically compelling reason for being sceptical about compensatory programmes of intervention: they are likely to affect a child's progress only temporarily. Any approach which ignores those roots of retarded development which may exist in cultural conflict between school and home, or which fails to build them into its methodology, seems to stand very little chance of affecting that development or that conflict in a productive way. An insistence on the supremacy of established professional values during the child's first steps in the formal educational world will not contribute to learning if that world is already alien to him in its superficial detail.

Linked with the British literature and research on disadvantage, which was quoted in Part 1, there has been a series of publications which connect disadvantage with deprivation. Briefly, the term 'cycle of deprivation' refers to social disadvantages being transmitted across generations, by parents to their children; deprivation appears to mean roughly the same as what we have generally termed disadvantage but with more evaluative undertones. A good illustration of the use of this concept in pre-school education is to be found in Sir Keith Joseph's address to the Pre-school Playgroup Association's 1972 conference, published by PPA.[1] A similar point of view is supported by the leader in the 21 September 1972 issue of *New Society*.[2] These statements carry the strong implication that poor material and social conditions are responsible in some sense for children's slow development and deviance. The compensatory argument is carried a stage further in the series of publications from the Department of Health and Social Security, particularly in the booklet entitled *The Family in Society: Preparation for Parenthood*[3] in the foreword of which strategies for breaking the cycle of deprivation are put forward; these strategies are clearly designed to bring parental care in deprived families into line with standards acceptable to the professional social, educational and medical workers in the field. Such interpretations of the research evidence exhibit very well what we have termed, in Chapter 2, a unilateralist approach to the problem: that is, they tend to conceive poor development along with other problems of maladjustment to formal learning, in terms only of poor preparation by the family, rather than a joint product of different cultures, preferring to attribute failure to a cycle of deprivation rather than to any unwillingness for professionals to accommodate different cultural values. They also illustrate the confusion, or overidentification, which is possible between the elements in the analysis of disadvantage which lead to designating areas or families in need, and the elements of the treatment plan which is proposed: they confuse, in other words, the method of analysing a problem with the development of techniques for dealing with it.

It is hopefully apparent that thorough appraisals of pre-school objectives should be made by those engaged in allocating places and devising curricula. Possibly such an appraisal will show that fairly short-term objectives are sufficient justification for providing a new range of experiences in a safe, welcoming and exciting environment. Where families are living in areas where housing and social conditions are difficult, then the need to introduce nursery units and other schemes becomes urgent if only to reduce the tensions and stress caused by the social environment. We do not deny the importance of supporting families in need but draw attention to the way in which the support is offered and maintained. If it is offered on the provider's terms, then there is a strong possibility that the potential self-realization for further intellectual growth, which each child and adult possesses, will be stunted. If the classes to which children who have received some form of early education eventually go do not adjust their standards and methods, then early gains will be diminished. The fusion of the family experience, through early education and well into full-time schooling must be seen as a gradual process starting at the nursery stage, or before, if the positive values of each situation are to be retained. It would appear that the movement of schools towards the community, on the community's terms, offers the best chance of a successful fusion taking place.

This may mean modifying existing resources by appointing staff to schools with specific tasks within the community and it certainly implies that facilities for extended use of buildings (including more caretaking and ancillary staff to maintain them), will be required if communities begin to use schools as resources. Other resources held by adult centres of education are only just being realized for the benefit of parents. The amorphous system of further and adult education facilities could be used much more closely with day schools to help meet the requirements of parents and teachers. The process of modifying existing resources to come to terms with a growing community awareness of the part families play in education also implies a modification of attitudes held by lay and professional people.

One of the more tenuous threads running through this book concerns training teachers, leaders, visitors and helpers as well as parents. New programmes for training staff who will be responsible for working with young children are being set up in colleges of education, teachers' centres and further education colleges. Training programmes offer an opportunity to examine attitudes and methodology afresh. They also offer time, some of which could be spent making first-hand observations of community life and in learning directly from the experiences of social workers. The balance of professional training often appears to be inappropriate for people who ultimately will be working with children and their parents. An example of a more realistic approach to providing a background of theory and experience for intending field workers can be seen in the Leicester Home-start programme where relationships play an important part in training the volunteers. Training should not be divisive, creating an élitist attitude between professional and lay persons. It should lead to a partnership by creating understanding and diagnostic attitudes between the enablers and the enabled.

Diagnosis implies an ability to identify needs in families. Not only do these vary between areas but also within areas. The social needs of individuals will have a strong influence on their educational responses. Whatever strategies are used in early education, whether family centres, nursery groups, self-help groups or visiting schemes, the various unmet social needs of families will impinge on educational work being carried out. There is no doubt that more opportunities for joint education and social service collaboration are provided at nursery and infant level than in other parts of the school system since more natural contact with parents is possible. An ideally effective situation to provide the best possible family service might be one in which a centre combines educational facilities for children aged from three to eight years with home visiting, medical and social services. But it would also require a strong community representation on the governing body, combined with a deliberate policy of scanning the surrounding area, in order to identify needs and to act in response to such needs by the multi-disciplinary team.

The screening process described in Part 1 of this volume would appear to fit more easily into the organization of a multi-purpose centre. The role of the teacher may, in such circumstances, become one of co-ordinating networks within the community as parents become more aware of their educative potential and help other adults and children. As the children become older and wean themselves away from their parents, teachers may enable small groups led by adolescents and other adults to operate in a controlled and structured way within the centre. Such a centre would be open to the community in order that individuals and groups would see it as a resource both from a therapeutic and an educative point of view. Its operation would be catalytic rather than ameliorative, contributory rather than compensatory.

While the idea of such a centre may be considered by the reader as a field worker's pipe-dream, it is not as remote from possibility as may appear at first sight. The component parts required are already operating independently within the community and within various servicing agencies. The major stumbling blocks for such development would appear to stem from well-established territorial rights which have been created by the servicing agencies and the reactions of the people receiving the service.

The challenge for the future lies in finding ways to encourage the energy and dynamism which exists within communities to be linked with imaginative flexible multi-purpose services which are locally based. The hope for the future exists in the potential of families to respond to the invitation of professional helpers and in combining their talents to rejuvenate their own world.

We have attempted, through this brief and somewhat prescriptive glance at the present and future, to summarize the thoughts contained in the previous chapters. Our hope is that the expansion of early education during the coming years will not be seen as the creation of yet another compartment, with specialist requirements, within the school system, but as a process which must reach across many boundaries. If social, educational and familial boundaries are reduced as a result then perhaps the pathway of opportunity for future generations may be less restricted continuously throughout their lives.

Notes

Preface

1 *Educational Priority*, A.H. Halsey (ed.), vol. 1, HMSO, 1972.
2 G.A.N. Smith (ed.), *Educational Priority*, vol. 4: *The West Riding Project*, HMSO, 1974.
3 *A Framework for Expansion*, DES White Paper, Cmnd 5174, HMSO, 1972; *Nursery Education*, Circular 2/73, DES.
4 *Nursery Education*, paras 19, 29.
5 Ibid., para. 16.

1 Criteria for success or failure

1 J.W.B. Douglas, *The Home and the School*, MacGibbon & Kee, 1964; B. Bernstein, 'Social Class and Linguistic Development; A Theory of Social Learning', in J.E. Floud, A.H. Halsey and C.A. Anderson, *Education, Economy and Society*, Free Press, 1961; A.H. Halsey, J.E. Floud and F.M. Martin, *Social Class and Educational Opportunity*, Heinemann, 1956.
2 Central Advisory Council for Education (England), *Children and their Primary Schools*, vol. 2, appendix 4, HMSO, 1967.
3 R.S. Peters (ed.), *Perspectives on Plowden*, Routledge & Kegan Paul, 1969.
4 H. Acland, 'Plowden in retrospect', *New Society*, 9 and 16 September 1971.
5 D.A. Pidgeon, *Expectation and Pupil Performance*, Almqvist & Wilksell, 1970.
6 R. Davie, N. Butler and H. Goldstein, *From Birth to Seven*, National Children's Bureau/Longman, 1972.
7 The risk referred to is peri-natal death, which occurred more readily when the mother smoked heavily during pregnancy, had severe toxaemia, was over 40, was having the fifth, or later, baby, or was from a low socio-economic group.
8 The data were gathered in 1965. An early report of a further follow-up study, when the children were 11 years old, appeared in 1973 by Peter Wedge and Hilary Prosser, *Born to Fail?*, Arrow, and is referred to later in this chapter.
9 It is beyond the scope of this discussion to probe the reaction to studies made in the USA, but interested readers are referred for reviews of the American experience in programmes for the disadvantaged to: A. Little and G.A.N. Smith, *Strategies of Compensation*, OECD, 1971. The relevant British programmes and strategies are reviewed at various points in the present volume.
10 J.S. Coleman *et al.*, *Equality of Educational Opportunity*, US Government Printing Office, Washington DC, 1966.
11 D. Denison (ed.), *A Pattern of Disadvantage*, NFER, 1972.

12 Wedge and Prosser, op. cit.
13 The impressionistic selection at the outset of the argument of three sets of circumstances, in terms of which other circumstances were assessed, affects only the extent of overlap found between them; whether the particular choices made have the effect of maximizing the overlap or not would depend on a closer examination of the data.

2 Intervention and innovation

1 Peter Wedge and Hilary Prosser, *Born to Fail?*, Arrow, 1973, p.55.
2 A.H. Halsey (ed.), *Educational Priority*, vol. 1, HMSO, 1972.
3 A well developed example of this approach is to be found in R.M. Wolf, 'The Identification and Measurement of Environmental Process Variables that are Related to Ability', Ph.D. thesis, Chicago University, 1964; and R.H. Dave, 'The Identification and Measurement of Environmental Process Variables that are Related to Educational Achievement', Ph.D. thesis, Chicago University, 1963.
4 For a review of the current state of developments see G.A.N. Smith and T. Smith, *Community Schools in England and Wales–A Review*, Occasional paper, Scottish Education Dept, 1974.
5 Chapter 6 reviews some current alternatives to groups.
6 W. Hodges, B. McCandless and H. Spicker, 'The Development and Evaluation of a Diagnostically Based Curriculum for Pre-school Psycho-socially Deprived Children', US Office of Education, 1967 (mimeographed).
7 M. Chazan, A.F. Laing and S. Jackson, *Just Before School*, Schools Council Research Project in Compensatory Education, Blackwell, 1971.
8 A.H. Halsey (ed.), *Educational Priority*, vol. 1, HMSO, 1972; and G.A.N. Smith (ed.), *Educational Priority*, vol. 4: *The West Riding Project*, HMSO, 1974.
9 C. Bereiter and S. Engelmann, *Teaching Disadvantaged Children in the Preschool*, Prentice-Hall, 1966.
10 D.P. Weikart, *Early Childhood Special Education for Intellectually Subnormal and/or Culturally Different Children*, High/Scope Educational Research Foundation, Ypsilanti, Michigan, 1971.
11 U. Bronfenbrenner, 'Is Early Intervention Effective', Paper, Cornell University, 1972.
12 See for instance R. Rosenthal and L. Jacobson, *Pygmalion in the Classroom*, Holt, Rinehart & Winston, 1968; D.A. Pidgeon, *Expectation and Pupil Performance*, Almqvist & Wiksell, 1970.
13 H. Acland, 'What is a bad school?', *New Society*, 9 September 1971, p.450.
14 R. Davie, N. Butler and H. Goldstein, *From Birth to Seven*, National Children's Bureau, Longman, 1972.
15 In the West Riding EPA project area parents who had attended one of the project's groups set up their own because the nursery their children were due to attend was not completed; this development has not, however, been evaluated or reported and ended when the children joined the nursery.
16 J. Barnes and H. Lucas, 'Positive Discrimination in Education: Individuals, Groups and Institutions', in T. Leggatt (ed.), *Sociological Theory and Survey Research: Institutional Change and Social Policy in Great Britain*, Sage, 1974.
17 *A Framework for Expansion*, DES White Paper, Cmnd 5174, HMSO, 1972.

3 A case study: the Red House pre-school groups

1 In G.A.N. Smith (ed.), *Educational Priority*, vol. 4, HMSO, 1975, the building and its uses are described during the period 1969-72.

2 Parents could bring younger siblings to the group but they had to accept total responsibility.
3 A box with a screen containing two sleeves through which the child feels, without seeing, objects.
4 S.H. Haskell and M.E. Paull, *Training in Basic Cognitive and Motor Skills*, ESA, Harlow, 1973.
5 Usually the room was used during the evenings by residents or special classes, who required a different set of furniture.
6 A film entitled 'Red House' in the BBC TV series 'Parents and Children' portrays an afternoon's group activities in the Centre and shows the teacher working with parents in the manner described above.
7 J. McVicker Hunt, *Intelligence and Experience*, Ronald, New York, 1961.
8 B.S. Bloom, *Stability and Change in Human Characteristics*, Wiley, 1964: 'about 50 per cent of intellectural development takes place between conception and age 4.'
9 The pre-school experiments in the West Riding are described in detail in G.A.N. Smith (ed.), *Educational Priority*, vol. 4, HMSO, 1975.
10 U. Bronfenbrenner's paper, 'Is Early Intervention Effective?', Cornell University, 1972, calls the conclusions based on Bloom's analysis into question, supported by follow-up data of intervention programmes in the USA.
11 G.A. Poulton, 'Educational Visiting in England 1973-4', unpublished M.A. thesis, Southampton University, 1975.
12 Erik Erikson, *Childhood and Society*, Hogarth Press, 1964, ch. 7, describes the eight stages of man.
13 Paper presented to a conference at the John Scott Health Centre, July 1971.
14 In this context we use the word 'teacher' to include 'pre-school leader', 'educational-visitor', 'playgroup supervisor'.
15 Leon Eisenberg, 'School Phobia: A Study in Communication of Anxiety', Paper read at the 113th annual meeting of the American Psychiatric Association, Chicago, 1957.
16 Infant schools and first schools in the United Kingdom usually admit children at 5 years or during their fifth year ('rising fives') and keep them until the age of 7 years in the case of infant schools and 8 or 9 years in the case of first schools.

4 A structured approach to early education

1 Central Advisory Council for Education (England), *Children and their Primary Schools*, (2 vols), HMSO, 1967 (The Plowden Report).
2 It is interesting to compare provision of nursery places by country. Table 1 gives a crude guide but does not describe the type of provision. The USSR nursery schools are nearly all full-time day-care establishments.
3 DES Circular 2/73 lists 70,000 places in 1971 available for 2-4 year olds in state-run nursery classes or schools. The figure of 250,000 children currently attending registered playgroups is an estimate by the PPA. All groups must be registered with the Department of Health and Social Security.
4 Brenda Crowe is the first National Adviser to the Pre-school Playgroups Association. Her book *The Playgroup Movement*, Allen & Unwin, 1973, is a report on the history, growth and activities of the movement.
5 Brian Jackson is director of the Childminding Research Unit. His article 'The childminders' appeared in *New Society*, 29 November 1973, p. 521.
6 A. Gesell, *The First Five Years of Life*, Harper & Row, 1940.
7 A.C. Munday-Castle and J. Anglin, 'The Development of Looking in Infancy', Paper presented at the Biennial Conference of the Society for Child

Table 1 State-provided nursery places in 1971, by country

	3 years (% of population)	4 years (% of population)
Belgium	80	90
USSR	20	20
France	50	80
Holland	-	80
England and Wales	5	35
Italy	50	50

Source: *A Framework for Expansion*, DES White Paper, Cmnd 5174, HMSO, 1972.

Development, Santa Monica, 1969.
8 J.S. Bruner, *The Relevance of Education*, Allen & Unwin, 1971.
9 Jean Piaget, *The Psychology of the Child*, Basic Books, 1969.
10 Henry Chauncey, *Soviet Pre-school Education*, vol. 1, Holt, Rinehart & Winston, 1969. An English translation of the official handbook for nursery staff in Soviet nursery schools, vol. 1 covers a programme of instruction. Vol. 2 embodies the psychological and pedagogical theory underlying the programme.
11 L. Vygotsky, *Thought and Language* (ed. and trans. by Eugenia Haufmann and Gertrude Vakar), MIT Press, 1962.
12 Gesell, *op. cit.*
13 Marion Blank, 'A Methodology for Fostering Abstract Thinking in Deprived Children', Paper presented to a conference on the 'Problems in the Teaching of Young Children', Toronto, March 1968. The paper includes the list of intellectual skills quoted on pp. 66-7. However, the notes accompanying the list are the authors'.
14 C. Bereiter and S. Engelmann, *Teaching Disadvantaged Children in the Pre-school*, Prentice-Hall, 1966.
15 Extracts from 'How shall the Disadvantaged Child be Taught?', M. Blank and F. Soloman, *Child Development*, 40(1), 1968, pp. 47-61.
16 Teresa Smith, 'Individual language work', in part 4 of the final report of the West Riding Educational Priority Area Project, Denaby Main, 1971.
17 The results of the West Riding EPA pre-school experiment formed part of the national experiment in five areas of the country. A report of the experiment is contained in A.H. Halsey (ed.), *Educational Priority*, vol. 1, HMSO, 1972. Further detailed accounts follow in vol. 4, G.A.N. Smith, 1975.
18 'West Riding EPA Project Early Education programme follow-up study', Unpublished research report, 1974, Social Science Research Council.
19 S.H. Haskell and M.E. Paull, *Training in Basic Cognitive and Motor Skills*, ESA, Harlow, 1973.
20 B.M. Caldwell, 'The Syracuse Early Learning Project', Paper presented at the American Psychological Association, September 1966.
21 I.J. Gordon, 'Early Child Stimulation Through Parent Education', Institution for the Development of Human Resources, College of Education, University of Florida, Progress Report 1968.
22 S. Gray and R. Klaus, 'Deprivation, Development and Diffusion', Address to American Psychological Association, September 1966.

23 D.P. Weikart and D. Lambie, Ypsilanti Carnegie Infant Education Project, Progress report, Michigan, February 1969.
24 A.D. Lombard, Interim Report, *Home Instruction Program for Pre-school Youngsters 1969-1970*, Center for Research in Education of the Disadvantaged, The Hebrew University of Jerusalem, 1971.
25 T. Kellaghan, 'A pre-school intervention project for disadvantaged children', *Oideas*, no. 10, Department of Education, Dublin, 1973.
26 Halsey, *op. cit.*
27 Longard, *op. cit.*
28 Ibid.
29 Final report of the West Riding EPA Project, section 5. 'The home visiting project' (1972) details the setting up and running of the first part of the programme. A summary of the full programme is contained in an unpublished paper 'Educational Visitor Programme—a Framework for Teachers, Parents and Children', 1974.
30 Cynthia Mitchell, *Time for School*, Penguin Educational, 1973.
31 John MacBeath, in the *Times Educational Supplement*, 11 January 1974, p. 4, 'Breaking up the egg crates', calls for flexible, imaginative alternatives in education.

5 Networks for learning: educative processes within the community

1 MacIver's definition, based on geographic location and common identity through work, religion, race, etc., would still be applicable in most of the Third World. It is important, however, to clarify to the reader that this chapter is concerned with communities in a modern urban, technological society. R.H. MacIver, *Community—A Sociological Study*, Macmillan, 1971.
2 G.H. Mead, *Mind, Self and Society*, University of Chicago Press, 1934.
3 A. O'Brien, 'Atheist in a foxhole', *New Statesman*, 3 January 1969.
4 P. Berger and T. Luckmann, *Social Construction of Reality*, Penguin University Books, 1971.
5 J. Coleman, *Community Conflict*, Free Press, 1957.
6 E. Durkheim, *The Division of Labour in Society*, Free Press 1966, rep.7.
7 D. Silverman, *The Theory of Organisations*, Heinemann, 1970.
8 Jacqueline Scherer, *Contemporary Community—Sociological Illusion or Reality?*, Tavistock, 1972.
9 J. Dewey, *The Public and its Problems*, Holt & Sons, 1929.
10 G. Taylor and N. Ayres, *Born and Bred Unequal*, Longman, 1969.
11 N. Dennis, F. Henriques and C. Slaughter, *Coal is our Life*, Tavistock, 1969.
12 Berger and Luckmann, *op. cit.*
13 Berger and Luckmann, *op. cit.*
14 Paulo Freire, *Celebration of Awareness*, Penguin, 1971.
15 A.H. Halsey (ed.), *Educational Priority*, Vol. 1, HMSO, 1972.

6 New directions in early education

1 *A Framework for Expansion*, DES White Paper, Cmnd 5174, HMSO, 1972.
2 G.A. Poulton, 'Educational Visiting in England 1973-4', unpublished M.A. thesis, Southampton University, 1975.
3 Extract from the Final Report, Section 5, 'Home-visiting', West Riding EPA Project, 1972.
4 Priority Area Playgroups Project appointed a visitor to work with child-minded groups in 1973. Described in more detail in the Annual Report (1974) of Priority Area Playgroups.
5 A.D. Lombard, Interim Report *Home Instruction Program for Preschool*

Youngsters 1969-1970, Center for Research in Education of the Disadvantaged, The Hebrew University of Jerusalem, 1971.

6 Margaret Harrison, *Home Start*, a report on its development from November 1973 to April 1974 for the Department of Health and Social Security, Leicester Council for Voluntary Service, April 1974.

7 Margaret Harrison, *Home Start*, a report on its development from May 1974 to July 1974, Leicester Council for Voluntary Service, August 1974.

8 Eric Midwinter, *Priority Education*, Penguin, 1972.

9 S. Lightman, 'The Playbus as a contribution to pre-school provision with special reference to the Lambeth Playbus', unpublished study for Diploma in Education, Institute of Education, London University, 1974.

10 Brian Jackson, 'The Childminders', *New Society*, 29 November 1973, p. 521.

11 See Eric Midwinter (ed.) *Preschool Priorities*, Ward Lock Educational, 1974, which contains a chapter by Margaret Johnson, describing the Centre.

12 The Centre for Research in Child Development, part of the Institute of Education, University of London.

13 Louise Sandler, Outline, describing the status of the Center for Preschool Services in Special Education Sponsored by the Franklin Institute Research Laboratories, Hahnemann Medical College and Hospital School District of Philadelphia.

14 Mia Kellmer Pringle, 'Total approach to under-fives', *Times Educational Supplement*, 1 June 1973, p.4.

15 Central Advisory Council for Education (England), *Children and their Primary Schools*, (2 volumes), HMSO, 1967.

16 Classes set up by the Extra-Mural Studies Department, University of Southampton, have been running during the academic year 1973-4, for parents living in three housing developments.

17 Poulton, *op. cit.*

18 The programmes mentioned are funded by various foundations and transmitted on public education channels in the USA without advertising sponsorship.

19 A. Joseph, *Preschool Playgroups in Areas of Social Need*, National Children's Bureau, 1972.

7 In conclusion

1 *The Importance of Playgroups in Education and the Social Services*, PPA, 1972.

2 'A Helping Hand', *New Society*, 21 September, 1972.

3 *The Family in Society: Preparation for Parenthood*, HMSO, London, 1974.

Index

Index